Historiography of Ancient Indian Law

Historiography of Ancient Indian Law

Paradigms from Imperialism to Postmodernism

SHIVA KANT TIWARI

RAWAT PUBLICATIONS
Jaipur • New Delhi • Bangalore • Guwahati • Kolkata

ISBN 978-81-316-0925-5

Published by
Prem Rawat for **Rawat Publications**
Satyam Apts, Sector 3, Jawahar Nagar, Jaipur 302 004 (India)
Phone: 0141 265 1748 / 7006 Fax: 0141 265 1748
E-mail: info@rawatbooks.com
Website: www.rawatbooks.com

New Delhi Office
4858/24, Ansari Road, Daryaganj, New Delhi 110 002
Phone: 011 2326 3290

Also at *Bangalore, Guwahati* and *Kolkata*

Typeset by Rawat Computers, Jaipur
Printed at Chaman Enterprises, New Delhi

Contents

Foreword

The British having entrenched themselves on the larger parts of India by the end of the eighteenth century were the first to take interest in the systematic study of India's past. Though the post renaissance spirit of inquisitiveness and the temptations of exotic East may had a role to play, the vigour and urgency to unravel the past of India were primarily the result of the compulsions of British imperialism. The East India Company which got transformed from a mercantile to a political entity within a short span of time, had no other option but to understand the customs and values of India. They began to apprise themselves with the longstanding socio-political ideas and institutions of India. This necessarily involved the perusal of the idea of state, notion of law, judicial procedures, property laws, family and marital practices as were prevalent in Indian society over the ages. Despite the fact that the British were not guided by the noblest of ideas, they not just laid the foundation of Indology in the nineteenth century but also set its initial trajectory. This was further enriched by the next generation scholars, both Indians and Westerners.

It needs no reiteration that historian is a product of his age and his views and perceptions of the past will have a tinge of his predisposition and philosophical inkling, sometimes obvious and at other times latent. Europeans, more prominently British, were no exception. Thus the imperialist historians if displayed no scruples in severely criticizing the society and polity of ancient India, their nationalist counterparts while eulogizing the past of India would often portray a make believe picture of India's past. If the former was providing legitimacy to imperial hegemony, the latter was supplying fodder to the national movement. The avowedly scientific and materialistic interpretation of past given by Marxist historians has its own share of dogmatism and determinism.

Since the establishment of the Royal Asiatic Society in 1784, there have been a plethora of works on the law and legal institutions of Ancient India. To begin with, *Dharmashastras* and *Smritis* were edited, translated and commented upon. *Manusmriti* coupled with *Yagnyavalkyasmriti* were considered to be the bedrock India legal system. Sooner than later, *Bhashya* (Commentaries) and *Nibandhas* (digests) were brought within the ambit and came to be regarded as important source of ancient Indian jurisprudence. Thus at present, there is no dearth of work on ancient Indian Law. However there is no denying the fact that there continues to be a paucity of works which endeavour to analyze the views and notions of scholars and historians who have written and commented upon ancient Indian legal system. In other words, historiography of ancient Indian law continued to be more or less a virgin terrain. Dr Shiva Kant Tiwari has undertaken the task to fill this gap through his book *Historiography of Ancient Indian Law: Paradigms from Imperialism to Postmodernism*.

In the present work, Dr Tiwari has meticulously examined and evaluated the different scholars and paradigms to study the law and legal institutions of ancient India. He has been rational and critical in his approach. Without being judgmental, he has compared and contrasted the basic tenets of different schools of historiography. Though the scope of the work is thoroughly comprehensive it never goes astray. Nor does it ever fail to betray the fact that this study is primarily analytical and comparative in nature. Perhaps the best part of any historiographical study is that it not only unravels the subtleties of the discussed topics but also brings forth the tone and temper of the age. Thus Dr Tiwari not only studies the perceptions of the historians but also enlightens us about the contours of socio-political discourse of the last two centuries. While perusing the book, one needs to be extremely cautious as it also reflects the British attitude towards India and the Indian response it generated. The present work is in many ways a noble undertaking. He deserves our unstinted support for this venture. We do hope that Dr Tiwari will continue to work in this field, so as to give impetus to further researches and inspire the budding scholars. At a time in which history is vociferously being appropriated by rival ideologies for political supremacy and a hegemonic narrative of the past is being thrust upon the masses, such historiographical studies provide the beacon of hope.

July 2017 **Dinesh Kr. Ojha**

Varanasi

Preface

Historiography is the interplay between text and context. But it is the historian that makes this interplay occur. Historian as a human being is destined to imbibe certain strings of likes and dislikes which not only determine the area of his research but also show the direction of his assumptions. The inherent contradiction with historiography is the fact that motivates a person to write history also germinate biases and subjectivity in his craft of history-writing. If interests are removed, subjectivity would be lessened; but then nobody would like to read or write history. Since, interests of the historians are different, the vision and versions of the history are poised to be different. The present work tries to illuminate this point with reference to the studies on legal ideas and institutions in ancient India.

Conventionally, Romans are credited to have excelled in the field of law while Indians in the field of spirituality. But if we look at the vast Sanskrit literature, we come across a strong and smooth tradition of indigenous science of jurisprudence in *Dharmshutra* and *Dharmshastra* (*Smriti)* texts followed by their *Bhashya* (commentaries) and *Nibandha* (digests). These legal works were not mere paper work or sheer intellectual exercises but were often accepted as the fundamentals of social behaviour. The significance of law in ancient India is evident by the fact that the law became synonymous with *Dharma*.

When British colonialism was making forays into Indian territories around the second half of 18th century, they perceived both the influence of law on Indian society and its importance for their administrative purposes. To some extent, they were inspired by new intellectual currents of contemporary Europe-like curiosity in discovering other societies, humanistic view of history, renewed interest in the remains. Consequently the British started to study, translate, and publish ancient Indian legal texts. But their interpretations of law and legal institutions often effused certain stereotypes like the superiority complex of British colonialism. Hence, with the rise of nationalist school of history writing from late 19th century onwards, imperialist verdicts on legal ideas and institutions in ancient India came to be challenged. From 1920s to 1930s, and afterwards, Marxist approaches, with a strong emphasis on materialism, were applied to study Indian history in general and its law in particular. When India got freedom in 1947, the imperialist versus nationalist debate lost its earlier charm and Marxists too began to be guided by new issues such as, social justice, economic reconstruction and secular politics. In this phase, many post-modern historians too studied the ancient Indian law and legal institutions.

This resulted in the output of innumerable interpretations and accounts of legal ideas and institutions in ancient India in modern historiography. But it is unfortunate that this aspect of ancient Indian studies could not be taken into account as comprehensively as it deserved. Reasons are obvious: students of ancient history almost confined themselves to the studies of original sources such as *Sutra* and *Smriti* texts, and researchers from law schools focused mainly on modern Hindu law as practised in independent India. How the historians owing allegiance to different schools of history-writing in the past two hundred years have viewed the law and legal institutions of ancient India remained almost outside the comprehensive contemplation. The present work, by studying the modern historiography of ancient Indian law, is aimed at filling this academic vacuum. It is a kind of work that bridges the gaps between ancient and modern periods of Indian history.

There is near absence of books on the present topic. We have plenty of books on either ancient Indian law or modern

Hindu law, but books dealing with the modern historiography of early Indian law are almost missing. However, some historians before writing their main chapters have discussed the earlier works on the various subjects of law. For example, U.N. Ghoshal in the 'General Introduction' of his book *A History of Indian Political Ideas* (1959, originally published in 1923) has examined briefly the views of many western indologists like Max Müller, Bloomfield and Willoghby, and so on, who had doubted the existence of secular political and legal ideas in India. Similarly, R.S. Sharma makes a brief perusal of earlier studies on various subjects related to legal ideas and institutions in the opening pages of his two books *Aspects of Political Ideas and Institutions in Ancient India* (first ed., 1959) and *Perspectives in Social and Economic History of Early India* (1983).

These works and some others of similar kind manifest a historiographical approach; but it is to be noted that this aspect is limited to either two–three pages or at most to a single introductory chapter. A book fully devoted to the historiography of ancient Hindu law including all its aspects such as political, social, family and proprietary laws has not been worked upon. Therefore, the present book entitled *Historiography of Ancient Indian Law: Paradigms from Imperialism to Postmodernism* seems to be the first of its own kind.

Since, the present work involves the study of historians' works on ancient Indian law, the instant methodology is 'secondary data review'. Primary sources of history are subordinated to the profuse use of secondary ones, i.e. modern historians' books. Any topic of law is studied in the light of its various interpretations, therefore comparison and critical evaluation is the hallmark of present work. Further, the unit of the study is particular school of history writing, not the individual historians. It is due to the fact that many historians belonging to same school of thought echo almost identical approaches. But it is to be remembered that no school of historiography is a single set of monolithic ideas, it always has variations and differences within called 'sub schools'. At times, even the individual historian is not entirely consistent in his interpretation. For instance, Henry Sumner Maine in his *Ancient Law* (1866) identifies the right to inherit ancestral property with the performance of obsequies in the sixth chapter (entitled 'Early History of Testamentary Succession') of his *Ancient Law* (1866) but in the seventh chapter (entitled 'Ancient and Modern Ideas Respecting Wills and Succession') of the same book, he finds this right being determined by birth. The present study highlights such discrepancies but concentrates principally on the fundamental differences among various schools in viewing the major topics of ancient Indian law.

Along with the schools of thoughts, the chronology too has been taken care of while perusing the historians of classical Hindu law. Historians have been studied in the sequence of historiographical development in India, i.e. imperialist, nationalist, Marxist and finally post-modern historians. This way of presentations shows that the passage of time has an impact over the tone and temper of history-writing. This is why after the withering away of imperialism and emergence of an almost decolonised world, western historians of post-war period changed their outlook and reflected a sensitive, holistic and more plausible interpretation of pre-modern Hindu law.

The book is divided into six chapters with germane sub-divisions, if necessary. The first chapter, entitled 'Modern Historiography with Special Reference to Ancient Indian Legal Studies' is a general survey of the rise and growth of modern historiography with its bearing on the study of ancient Indian legal ideas. In this chapter, various phases and trends of modern historiography such as Renaissance, Enlightenment, Romanticism, Positivism along with contributions of many philosophers of history have been discussed. Further, it has been described that how the imperialist historiography, which was the first instalment of modern historiography in India condemned society, polity, religion, laws, customs and manners of 'Hindus'. But from the later half of the 19th century, nationalist historians began to glorify these aspects and tried to establish the sound traditions of jurisprudence, welfare state and constitutional monarchy in early Indian context. Marxists criticized both the imperialists and nationalists and applied materialistic approaches to study the ancient Indian history in general and its law in particular. In the last part of the chapter, it has been tried to explain that the post-modern historian tried to analyse the ancient Indian law with epistemological methods of post-structuralism.

The second chapter, 'The Notion of Law in Ancient India: Reflections from Modern Historians', is an analysis of the ancient Indian notion of law as understood by modern historians. In this chapter, historians' perceptions related to different aspects of the concept of law, such as: nature, sources, divisions and limitations of law are critically examined. Imperialists either questioned the prevalence of systematic concept of law or viewed it as a stagnant, religio-customary rule. Conversely, nationalists projected corpus of sacred and dynamic law. Subsequently, Marxist vision of the notion of law in relation to socio-economic processes and post-modernist account of the subject have been evaluated. The post-modern writer Robert Lingat (*The Classical Law of India*, 1973) viewed ancient and early medieval Indian law as an evolutionary phenomenon and regarded *commentaries* and *digests* of medieval period as 'true juridical science'. Similarly, J.D.M. Derrett (*Religion, Law and the State in India*, 1968) countered the 'overbearing influence of religion' on Hindu law and Donald R. Davis Jr. (*The Sprit of Hindu Law*, 2010) advocated the need of Hindu law to avoid the 'total depersonalization' of European legislation. These assumptions by post-modern Indologists undisputedly show a paradigm shift in western approaches to study the legal aspects of Indian history.

The third chapter, 'Interpretations of Social Legislation in Ancient India', is an assessment of historians' views on social and family laws. Indeed, social legislation is a very vast and open-ended area. In order to avoid unnecessary ramification and expansion, this chapter is categorically sub-divided into three heads 'Creation of Social Order', 'Marital Laws' and 'Sonship and Adoption'.

Imperialists assumed that caste system marked by vast gap in privileges and disadvantages between *Brahmans* and *Shudras* was a Brahmanic contrivance and this constitutes the hallmark of Indian society. They also projected the religious and tribal character to be present in the marital and sonship laws of Hindus. But nationalists pronounced that *Varna* system was created out of difference in natural abilities and functional efficiency, and Dharmasastric theories of *Jatyutkarsha* (upward revision of caste) and *Jatyapakarsha* (downward change of the caste) always ensured enough flexibility. Different forms of marriages and sonship including adoption, claimed nationalists, denote different stages of social progress and an inclusively liberal nature of pre-modern Hindu law. Marxists are close to imperialists in criticizing caste system, but they interpret its origin materialistically and see its deep impact on the institutions of marriage and sonship. This chapter elaborates all these opinions and also betrays that post-modernists adopted a more comprehensive standpoint of the subject.

The fourth chapter entitled, 'Proprietary Laws in Ancient India: An Interpretational Insight', is aimed at surveying vividly historians' views on three crucial topics of ancient Indian law: Property and Ownership, Succession and Inheritance and Women's Property Rights. James Mill, leading the imperialist front, alleged that the high magnitude of legislations on the topics of 'Rescission of Sale and Purchase' and 'Deposits' shows Hindus' immature commercial consideration and insecure society respectively. With regard to inheritance laws, he criticised the qualification criterion for sons, its 'patriarchal' feature and also censured women's 'exclusion' from property rights.

It has also been described that how nationalists led by P.N. Sen (*The General Principles of Hindu Jurisprudence*, 1918) and P.V. Kane (*History of Dharmasastra*, Vol. III, 1946) responded to imperialist pronouncements. In their opinion, the law on rescission of sale was created to protect from 'hasty and inconsiderate bargains'. They, in the light of *Mitakkshara* rules, countered the stereotype of religious efficacy in inheritance laws and highlighted provisions for women's property rights, mainly *Stridhana*. Marxists studied the notion of individual property with its relation to class-divided society and painted women as a kind of 'movable property' and thereby being incapable of holding 'immovable property'. Besides, a number of historians followed by a number of interpretations on a range of issues related to proprietary laws have been discussed in this chapter. It has also been proposed that Derrett's essay entitled,

'An Indian Contribution to the Study of Property' marks one of the best critiques of the subject.

'The Laws of State Affairs: Historiographical Perspectives' which stands to be the fifth chapter is sub-divided into four heads: 'Origin and Nature of State', 'State as a Source of Law', 'Revenue Regulations' and 'International Laws'. Initiating the research in the field, imperialists viewed the state in India as an extension of 'Oriental Despotism'. They propagated the 'uncertain' and 'oppressive' taxation policy of 'Hindu' states and the absence of international laws to guide diplomatic business. Contrary to this, nationalists described state in ancient India as welfare orientated, organic entity promoting the prosperity and well-being of its people. State came to be described as a source of law also since it used to pass decrees and royal edicts for internal administration. Nationalists asserted that 'Hindu' taxation policy was reasonable and equitable, and inter-state relations were based on sound international laws.

Marxists like R.S. Sharma and Romila Thapar studied the rise and growth of state as a long-drawn process which due to suitable material background got a definite shape in sixth century B.C. Apart from elaborating all these points of historiographical interest, views of J.D.M. Derrett, who applied both the practical and ideological standpoints to study the state in ancient India, have been examined.

The sixth chapter of the book 'Judicial and Penal Laws: Historians' Observations' is divided into two sub-sections: 'Laws of Judicature' and 'Penal Laws'. It has been attempted to delineate that imperialists assumed that the king in ancient India had concentrated all the powers including the judicial one. James Mill doubted the prevalence of written evidence and perceived 'severity' and 'retaliation' in the Hindu law of punishment. Nationalists claimed the supremacy of law and maintained that judiciary always remained separate from the executive. They also highlighted the existence of written evidences and documents as a proof in judicial courts. To interpret some provisions for harder punishment, they resorted to the Hindu principle that no guilty should go unpunished, and explored similar laws in other cultures. Marxists in their turn underlined the *varna* and caste element in the administration of justice and evidence laws. These assumptions including many others with their merits and limitations along with post-modern interpretations have been fully discussed in the chapter.

Conclusively, it can be observed that there was direct interaction among various schools of historiography. Historians of one particular school seem to comment on the formulations of others which gave rise to diverse paradigms in the study of ancient Indian law. As there was 'stimulus–response' pattern in the politics, particularly during Indian national movement, history-writing progressed in the similar model of propositions and counter-propositions. It is hoped that scholars will undertake resembling research on the other aspects of ancient India and thereby examine the paths and lanes of modern historiography.

Acknowledgement

Writing a book on historiographical subject has always been a daunting task, as the area is open ended and involves cross currents of opinions. On 5 August 2016, I met Romila Thapar at Jawaharlal Nehru University (JNU), New Delhi and discussed about these problems in approaching historiography. She advised me to focus on the study of different interpretations and refrain from drawing any final conclusion. This suggestion helped me from being trapped in an extremely ramified area of historiography. If I succeeded in my endeavour, it is due to a series of such suggestions and guidance from a host of learned people.

I express my deep sense of gratitude to Professor V.L. Dharurkar (President's Nominee for JNU and Emeritus Professor, BAMU, Aurangabad) for providing me insights of the philosophy of history and its relation with the craft of history-writing. Professor Dinesh Kr. Ojha (Department of Ancient Indian History Culture-AIHC and Archaeology, Banaras Hindu University (BHU) Varanasi) introduced me to the field of historiography during pursuit of my MA and PhD courses from BHU. His teaching made me holistic towards history and thus saved from being swept away with particular ideology. I am extremely grateful to him also for writing the Foreword to the book and thereby unveiling its methodological and conceptual contours for the readers. Special thanks are due to my esteemed teachers at Dept. of AIHC & Archaeology, BHU, Varanasi particularly Professor Vibha Tripathi and Professor Sita Ram Dubey whose academic standing and overall personality have always inspired me. I am equally indebted to my revered teacher from University of Allahabad Professor Sushmita Roy (Department of English and Modern European Languages) for her constant support in more than one way. I also feel indebted to my teachers at Adya Prasad Inter-College (Dhoos-Koraon, Allahabad) particularly late Tilak Dhari Vishwakarma for my foundational learning.

I am beholden by the help given by a number of people at several levels during the completion of book. These include Advocate Hiraji Gaikwad (Bombay High Court), Ashish Shukla (Indian Council of World Affairs-ICWA, New Delhi), Animesh Prakash (Centre for Buddhist Studies, University of Hong Kong, Hong Kong), Jayant Kumar (Dept. of AIHC & Archaeology, BHU), and Sandip Singh (Bora Institute of Management Sciences, Lucknow) among many others. I offer my sincere thanks to the librarian and entire staff of the Departmental and Central library, Law College Library, BHU, Varanasi and JNU Library, New Delhi, for providing me required source material regularly.

It appears needless to formally thank my family members. Still, I recall the blessings of my mother Chandrakali Tiwari and father Baij Nath Tiwari who despite several domestic hardships sustained my education. My six elder brothers namely, Kamla Shankar Tiwari, Vishnu Datta Tiwari, Hari Krishna Tiwari, Vijay Shankar Tiwari, Laxmi Kant Tiwari and Vidya Kant Tiwari, all working in different capacities across the country have always supported me at all occasions and minimised my household liabilities. Besides, I am indebted to all other members of my family particularly wife Meenakshi and newly born son Shashwat who have been helpful to me in their own ways.

Last but not least, I thank Pranit Rawat and his team at Rawat Publications, Jaipur for extending all the assistance in publishing the book. Despite all efforts to make the book error free, there may remain some gaps. Any gap or imperfection pointed out to me on *shivakant81942bhu@gmail.com* would be beneficial.

July 2017
New Delhi

Shiva Kant Tiwari

1

Modern Historiography

Special Reference to Ancient Indian Legal Studies

'Man is a social animal' has become a cliché. Man is a historical animal, though as true, is yet to be understood.[1] Man is the product, bearer and maker of history. This explains the very fact that the history is part and parcel of individual's and community's mental 'being' and becoming. All this is considered the *'history as memory'* which is natural and almost an organic kind of phenomenon. However, the thing which academia is concerned about is the *history as text* – or written history – which has to be cultivated with the special efforts by enlightened people. This active, conscious and deliberate part of history is historiography. Thus, by its very nature, historiography is not only the craft of recording past, but also the reconstruction of historical thought. This led Butterfield to observe that historiography is the study of the development of man's sense for the past.[2]

The craft of history-writing or historiography has always been present in different forms in almost all civilizations of ancient world namely, Greek, Roman and Chinese. In India, an oral tradition of historical sense, as in the *gatha* (hero-lauds) and *narasamsi* (praises celebrating men) existed in a nebulous and amorphous form even in Rig Vedic times. To these were added in the later Vedic age and after, other forms of quasi-historical compositions the *akhyana* (historical narrative), *itivratta* (occurrence), *purana* (ancient folk lore) and *itihasa* (verily, thus it happened), etc. We also come across the individual writers of *Vamsa* and *Charita*, such as Bana Bhatta and Bilhna, who have dealt with the historical content of their choice. Kalhna's *Rajatrangini* and his objective approach elevate him to the first true historian of India in every sense. In medieval period, the Indian historiography was further enriched immensely because of prolific patronage of chroniclers by most rulers.

But most of the pieces of pre-modern history-writing, though commendable in various aspects, embrace some weaknesses such as hyperbolic expression, poetic embellishment, subjectivity, mythological models, and theological shackles, etc. The credit to exonerate history-writing from all these dogmas and to reshape it as an independent rigorous branch of learning, goes to the emergence of modern Indian historiography.

Rise and Growth of Modern Historiography

Modern historiography, like any other modern phenomenon, is very much associated with the rise and growth of modernity in Europe. The first development that marked the beginning of modern age is Renaissance. Renaissance is the period of Europian intellectual and cultural reawakening in 15th and 16th which occurred owing to its new geographical discoveries and renewed interest in Graeco-Roman classicism. It preached the values of ancient humanism, this-worldliness, reasoning, etc., and replaced the pessimistic classical view of the future with an optimistic one. Religion which had till now stifled the growth of history lost its central position and gave way to critical and dispassionate analysis of past. The new belief in man's free will and limitless capacity eroded the medieval notion of devine intervention and surrendering to faith. It paved the way for the naturalistic interpretation of 'cause and effect'. Lorenzo Valla's famous exposé declaring the 'donation of Constantine' a forgery marks the first achievement of textual criticism in historiography. The Florentine philosopher and historian, Machiavelli and Guicciardini respectively, heralded a new historiography with stress on accuracy of detail, critical examination of sources, secular and political argumentation, et cetera. This renaissance spirit, which played a crucial role in shaping modern historiography, was further strengthened during Enlightenment or the 'Age of Reason'.

The term Enlightenment – *Eclaircissement* in French – signifies 'a victory brought by the forces of light over those of darkness.'[3] This atmosphere of victory was facilitated by the scientific revolution of 17th and 18th centuries and the intellectual revolution led by a secular class of philosophers such as: Francis Bacon, René Descartes, John Locke, Immanuel Kant, Voltaire, and others. Enlightenment emphasized supremacy of reason and scientific outlook to view the present and the past. This movement influenced modern historiography deeply by way of its revolt against religion, secularization of history, unity of human history, and the idea of endless progress for mankind.

The Enlightenment redefined the methodology of historiography as well. It began to establish that the proper way of studying the past was to develop an attitude of disinterestedness, or non-attachment towards it. A critical and dispassionate approach towards history was propounded. The documents including the oriental texts were rationally analysed and translated. The impact of climate, religion, ideals and values of any society of people were supposed to be the important factors in the causation of history.

Utilitarianism stands to be one of the most dominant intellectual currents under the broad canopy of Enlightenment era. This school, as revealed by its proponents – Bentham and J.S. Mill, asserts that the sole parameter to judge any tradition or institution should be its utility for people. On this humanist criterion, utilitarian thinkers condemned many ancient societies across the globe. For the utilitarians, 'rule of law' is the most effective measure to revolutionize the change in any society. A government based on the 'rule of law' must fulfil the ideal of 'maximum good of maximum number', they stressed. Seeing the absence of such features, scholars like Mill criticized the eastern civilizations in general and Indian culture in particular. Lord Macaulay called Indian society a backward one and advocated for British government's role in modernizing Indians.

Parallel to intellectual developments, European economic systems too underwent drastic changes. Technological advancements and increased demand for goods due to expanding colonisation paved the way for industrial revolution in the middle of eighteenth century and onwards. Big industries employing organized labour and raw material extracted from colonies began to produce profuse amount of goods. The new city-centric capitalist economy emerged but its benefits were distributed skewedly in favour of big merchants and factory-owners, leaving the large section of society deprived. Vast population migrated from villages to cities in search of livelihoods. But in addition to low wages and difficult working conditions, they had to cope with alienation. On the other side, natural resources of colonies were exploited inexorably.

This bewildering social and economic change made some people rethink the efficacy of science and reason in solving the problems of humanity, and to reconsider ancient traditions. Such a movement, signifying a reaction against intense rationalism of Enlightenment and relying heavily upon emotion, imagination and fantasy is known as Romanticism.

Romanticism – often regarded as the 'Age of Feeling' – subordinated skepticism, rationalism and intellectualism of the Enlightenment to faith and feeling, imagination and mystery, sentiment and romance. Jean Jacques Rousseu was the inspirer, the messiah of the Romantic Movement. He impugned the Enlightenment belief in human progress and gave his famous call 'back to nature' by asserting that progress is nothing but degeneration.

Immnuel Kant's *Critique of Pure Reason* was replaced with Rousseau's *New Heloise* (1761) which proclaimed the primacy of feeling over reason. J.G. Herder, the harbinger of Romantic Movement in Germany, directly inserted the romanticist tenets in historiography. He, in his *One More Philosophy of History* (1774), opposed the rationalism in history writing and tried to demonstrate that nature and history obey a uniform system of laws.

The biggest contribution made by romanticists to the historiography is the widening of the scope of history. The romantic love of the mysterious and the unknown contributed to a new interest in strange and distant societies and civilizations such as the Chinese, Indian, Persian, Arabic, and so on. Contrary to the recent origin of Enlightenment's 'reason', 'general will' as Rousseau conceived it, has always and everywhere existed. R.G. Collingwood rightly observes that 'the principle upon which Rousseau explained history was a principle which could be applied not only to the recent history of civilized world but to the history of all races and all times'.[4] This is why the field of study Indology, which was gerinated during Enlightenment age, received not only the greatest impetus but also a sound sympathetic and respectful treatment by the Romanticist scholars like William Jones, Thomas Munro and Mountstuart Elphinstone.

But while creating new interest in history, Romanticist historiography caused many baneful effects simultaneously, such as mystification of life and history, treating history as literature (as seen in Thomas Carlyle's works), subordination of content to style, nostalgic love for past ages, dangerous theories of race and culture, chauvinistic-nationalist approaches, et cetera. It was these loopholes due to which the romantic school could give way to positivism.

Just as Romanticism was the reaction to Enlightenment, Positivism was a reaction to Romanticism.[5] Positivism is the 'belief that the method of natural sciences provides the principle, or even the sole method for the attainment of true knowledge'.[6] Being influenced by the developments in natural sciences, this school of thought endeavoured to make history as objective and rational as science is. Leopold Von Ranke was a staunch supporter of positivism. He proposed the notion of factual exactitude, and advised historians to describe the events as these actually had happened. The task of historian is not to pass judgment or moralize the reader, but, as Ranke puts it, 'simply to show how it really was'.[7]

The French philosopher Auguste Comte was the high priest of positivism. He was the secretary of Saint Simon, the French radical, who rejected all metaphysical approaches and established 'gravitation' as the model of systematic comprehension and ultimate unity across every branch of knowledge.

Accordingly, Comte emphasized not only on the sanctity of facts as Ranke had done, but also on framing of historical laws analogous to the laws of the natural sciences. By tracing the connection between facts, between events, Comtean positivism proved itself to be a valuable corrective to the Rankean approach to history. The Rankeans were so concerned with the unique events and exact details, that at times this work seemed completely shapeless.[8]

Comte termed history as 'social physics'. He was influenced by Vico's *Scienza nouva* (1725) especially by his idea of spiral recurrence of periods and general characterization of history. Such a concept rested on the premise that historical events followed a fixed pattern which was understandable. By discerning the causal connection between past happenings, certain laws and principles could be framed. With the help of these laws, predictions about the future could also be made. In this way positivism replaced the sensational and fanciful views with the new rational and scientific concepts in historiography. It was the result of the positivist confidence in the 'Age of Science' which made J.B. Bury asserts that 'history was simply a science no less no more'.

Karl Marx is said to have raised positivistic outlook in history to a high philosophical level, that is, historical materialism. Marx out-distanced all other philosophers in developing an approach to historiography with its thrust in general laws and broad patterns for interpretations.[9]

In the first phase of twentieth century, renewed interest in philosophy showed itself in a kind of overarching philosophical history as represented by Oswald Spengler and Arnold Toynbee, as well as in a reconsideration of the nature of history as seen in the work of Bernedetto Croce and R.G. Collingwood. Spengler and Toynbee were philosophers of history, the theme of their philosophizing being the past itself, for which the First World War (1914–1918) in part provided the stimulus. Both tried to detect a grand design in history and aimed at revealing what they thought were general cyclic laws behind the rise and fall of civilisations. (Though Spengler has used the term 'culture'.)

Croce and Collingwood represented the idealistic view of history which was seeded greatly in Hegel's philosophy of 'Dialectic Idealism'. These two men provided a philosophical justification of the relativist mood in historiography by looking at the historians' own present surrounding. The celebrated aphorism by Croce that 'All history is contemporary history'[10] means that the past (History) has existence only in minds of contemporaries (Historians). Similarly Collingwood's *Idea of History* proposed that 'The history of thought and therefore all history is the re-enactment of past thought in the historians' own mind.'[11]

In addition to these major schools of historiography, there were some minor intellectual streams, which affected the tone and temper of modern historiography. There were evangelicals like John Shore and Charles Grant (*Observations on the State of Society among the Asiatic Subjects of Great Britain* (1798) who were attracted towards the past of India as well. Backed by the missionaries, they believed that Christianity would succeed in India only when the religion, values, customs, traditions were understood by the proselytizers. They justified British rule in India as a 'divine deliverance' to redeem a condemned humanity; and also tried to change Indian society through conversion, education and medication.

In 1859, the publication of *Origin of Species* by Charles Darwin changed the worldview of scientists and historians alike. It attacked the concept of 'creationism' in life sciences and inspired the historians to look at the evolutionary nature of socio-political institutions and cultural traditions, instead of treating them of abrupt origins. At the same time, 'survival of the fittest' came to be used as the moral justification for imperialist conquest over the colonies in Asia and Africa.

In Indian context, modern historiography is the reflection of above-mentioned schools and thought patterns. But since India was a British colony, the main local issue – imperialism versus nationalism dominated historical writing. Marxism, which began to influence historical studies in India from 1930s and 1940s onwards is entirely different on the issue of imperialism and nationalism, and is marked by its own unique interpretive models. Accordingly, the modern Indian historiography can be divided in to three broad categories:

- Imperialist Historiography
- Nationalist Historiography
- Marxist Historiography

Imperialist Historiography

The emergence of modern historiography in India is an intellectual development of the late 18th century under the aegis of British imperialism. Imperialism is basically a policy of extending the mother country's political and economic control, but at the same time it also tries to establish a cultural supremacy over the conquered nation. With this inborn motif of imperialism, imperialist history-writing in India can be understood.

After the successive victories in the Battles of Plassey (1757) and Buxar (1764), East India Company started annexing larger parts of the India and thereby converted itself into a political power from a mere mercantilist company. After the one-sided Pact at Allahabad (1765), the British administrators and governors realized that an acquaintance with traditional Indian laws, politics, customs, and religion was necessary in strengthening their administrative reach and hereby strengthening economic exploitation. This perception is clearly highlighted in a letter to N. Smith by Warren Hastings dated 4 October 1784 wherein he says,

> 'every accumulation of knowledge, and especially such as is obtained by social communications with the people over whom we exercise a dominion founded on the right of conquest is useful to the state ... it lessons the weight of the chain by which the natives are held in subjection'.[12]

Familiarity with Indian culture and religion could minimize the foreignness of Britons and ensure them a kind of local social acceptability. For that, the knowledge of Indian languages – mainly Sanskrit – was a must.

Besides the inherent imperialist compulsion, there was an increasing Enlightenment trend of studying philology, science and humanities with new approaches across Europe. Many philosophers were in search of new culture and societies in order to check and justify their newly evolved hypothesis and values of universality, rationality and catholicity. Majority of the company officials, such as Jones, Colebrooke and Wilson were trained in the classical tradition of Europe. Their appointment by East India Company in India gave them the opportunity to revitalize their academic pursuit with Sanskrit literature. So, as Romila Thapar writes, administrative and scholarly interests coalesced,[13] and this paved way for the beginning of modern history-writing in India.

The last quarter of the 18th century, in relation to the progress of historical research in India, centres round the personalities of the period of Warren Hastings (1772–85), the first governor general who is credited to have understood the direct relation between knowledge of Indian culture and efficient administration first.[14] Under his patronage, some local Brahamanas compiled *Vivadarnavsetu* (Across the Sea of Litigation), a compendium of Hindu laws for judicial purposes. Sir William Jones, who stands as the father of 'British Indology', established The Asiatic Society in 1784 in Calcutta, which proved to be the milestone of indological studies by serving as the forum for translation and publication of ancient Indian texts.

Jones was able to create an impact on continental scholars by his translation of Sanskrit classics and juristic literature. These included *Sakuntala* and *Ritu Samhara* (1792) by Kalidas, *Manusmriti: The Ordinances of Manu* (1794) the *Gita Govind* of Poet Jaydeva and *Hitopadesha* (posthumously, 1799). It was the impact of these publications that India came to be treated as the primary object of investigation in the first quarter of the 19th century. This manifested itself in the growth of German school of Sanskrit and Indology in a number of universities.[15] Jones as a philologist discovered a close affinity among languages belonging to the family called Indo-European. After him, H.T. Colebrooke contributed immensely to the indology and became logical successor to Jones. Colebrooke published his famous law book entitled *A Digest of Hindu Law on Contracts and Succession* (1798).

The most revered name among the early Indologists is that of German scholar Max Müller who renamed himself as *Moksha Mula*, denoting his love for Indian values. Though he never visited India but contributed a lot in the growth of Oriental studies, particularly in field of comparative philology. He studied deeply the ancient Sanskrit texts namely *Vedas* and *Upanishadas*, and presented many publications such as *India: What can It Teach Us? History of Ancient Sanskrit Literature, Sacred Book of the East* (SBE) series, etc. The publication of *Sacred Book of of the East* series was a major step in the direction of discovering the past of India. This series made available in English the *vedas*, the *upanishadas*, the Buddhist and the Jaina canonical works. But it was the critical edition and translation of various *Dharmasutras* and *Smritis* by Indologists like Georg Bühler which proved to be of immense help in knowing the polity and laws of ancient India.

The study of Sanskrit language and literature not only gave shape to the discipline of comparative philology, but also became the source material for the reconstruction of ancient Indian society. This led Max Müller to romanticize India's past (chiefly Vedic period) and praise its cultural achievements namely, religion, value-systems, philosophy, grammar, metaphysics, etc. But regarding the ancient Indian political ideas and institutions, he seemed driven by typical imperialist assumptions. He maintains that Indians were a nation of philosophers and they were too engrossed in the metaphysical speculation and other worldliness to consider material world. He writes-

> 'while other nations as Egyptians, Greeks, and Romans ... have their certain periods, culminated on the political horizon of the world, India has moved in such a small and degraded circle of political existence that it remained almost invisible to the eyes of other nations'.[16]

By far the most influential theory to emerge from Indological studies in the nineteenth century was the Theory of Aryan Race. The words *airii* and *arya* from the Iranian Avestan and Vedic Sanskrit texts were given a racial connotation, as referring to the race of Aryans. But the identification of language and race was a fallacy ... since in the texts it merely refers to an honored person of high status.[17]

So, intellectual and imperial, both the elements seemed to have pervaded the indological studies by Europeans. O.P. Kejariwal observes that there were two different worlds in this period, one of science, knowledge and research and second was of administration and imperialism. Though all Indologists cannot be regarded as the agents of imperialism but they certainly embraceed imperialist approach to some extent in their ancient Indian studies.[18]

The typical imperialist vision of Indian past came from the Utilitarian philosophers like James Mill in the early decades of nineteenth century. Among the early British historians, James Mill was the most important one. His famous book *The History of British India* (1818–20) in three volumes is regarded as the first comprehensive history-book as it covers all aspects: society, polity, religion, law, etc. Mill neither visited India nor knew any of its languages, but his historical concepts about India's past somehow proved to be the basic assumptions of imperialist historiography.

With his utilitarian outlook, Mill gave an account of India's past which as a whole was an object of great contempt for him. In his view, Indian society was inert and stratified into castes which were characterized by the stark differences in the rights and privileges between the Brahmans and the Sudras. Mill observes: 'As much as the Brahman is an object of intense veneration, so much is the Sudra an object of contempt.'[19]

Apart from society, religion is said to have pervaded all facets of life in the oriental world. It was the common imperialist view about the East and India. So was the belief of Mill who opined:

> 'No where among Mankind have the laws and ordinances been more exclusively referred to the divinity, than by those who instituted the theocracy of Hindustan. The plan of society and government, the rights of persons and things, even the customs, arrangements, and manners of private and domestic life, everything in short is established by divine prescription'.[20]

The next recurring theme in the Mill's writing and imperialist historiography in general is the prevalence of 'Oriental Despotism' in India. Indeed, this idea can be traced to Aristotle when he pointed out that oriental rule is autocratic in nature. Thomas Hill Green stated that 'the empires of the East are in the main, tax-collecting institutions. They exercise coercive power on their subjects of the most violent kind'.[21] Treading the same path, Mill expressed that among the Hindus, according to the Asiatic model, the government was monarchial and absolute.[22] The other points which find echo in imperialist historiography are that Indians lacked the sense of history, feeling of national solidarity and material speculation.

The practical implications of these imperialist stereotypes were very dangerous to the demand for self-government in India. If Indians were essentially philosophers absorbed in the problems of the spiritual world, it followed that their material world should be managed for them by their imperialist masters. If Indians were accustomed to autocratic rule and never had any idea of nationhood, state or self-government, the British Governors' dictatorship was the further extension of that tradition. Mill's *History of British India* became a textbook on India at the Haileybury College, where the British officers of the Indian Civil Services were trained. Through this book, British officers began to perceive colonial rule as a boon and historical need for 'backward' India, instead of realizing the cruel and exploitative nature of British imperialism.

Notwithstanding the tones of utilitarians, there were historians like John Malcom, Mounstuart Elphinstone, Peter Auber, John Clark Marshman, who viewed Indian history with sympathetic and comparatively sensitive perception. Elphinstone's famous book *The History of India*, first published in 1893, is a typical example representing Romanticist account of India's past. He rejected the Enlightenment view of unity of human history across the globe and asserted that traits and characters of societies depend on the different surroundings, so vary from region to region and time to time. This led Elphinstone to study the past of India by taking into account its peculiarities and uniqueness.

Elphinstone was perhaps the first historian who felt the need of a chronological framework for the history of ancient India. Dismissing the traditional Hindu concept of the four *yugas* extending over a period of more than four million years, he started the history of the Hindus from the date of compilation of Rig Veda. He happened to be one of the earliest European scholars who believed that Indians did possess a sense of history which was not necessarily similar in its linearity to that of ancient Greeks and Chinese. He took a balanced view while studying the society, polity and laws of ancient India. In his opinion caste system which is marked by the predominance of Brahamanas over all other castes is the most prominent feature of Indian society, but he also claimed, 'the institute of caste, ... has by no means so great an effect in obstructing the enterprise of individuals as European writers are apt to suppose.[23] Even though he held that criminal law of Hindus is very rude, still highlighted its better side, and affirmed 'the laws of civil judicature are very superior to the penal code, and indeed are much more rational and matured than could well be expected of so early an age'.[24]

In the later half of the 19th century, Elphinstone's romanticist account tried to lessen the impact of Mill's historical conclusions; but the changing policies of British Imperialism hindered its success. The '1857 rebellion' again infused racial and social disgust in the minds of colonial rulers in the form of revenge. The Britishers gave up policies of social reforms, and, instead, promoted the reactionary forces present in Indian society to diffuse nationalist spirit. For that purpose, Mill's account of Indian past was more useful than that of Elphinstone.

In the beginning of the twentieth century, Vincent Smith, a die-hard imperialist, produced his comprehensive work *Early History of India* (1904). It is mainly the chronological overview of rise and fall of prominent dynasties of Indian history. Contrary to his claim of objectivity, Smith effuses imperialist bias at several occasions. Commenting upon the close affinity between history and religion in ancient India, he remarks, 'The works of ancient writers from which our historical data are extracted don't ordinarily profess to be histories, and are mostly religious treatises of various kinds.'[25] D. Lorenzen has rightly regarded Smith's *Early History of India* as the Mature Imperialist school of Indian historiography.[26] *Cambridge History of India* series (1922) treaded the same path of imperialist assumption with some modifications. In it, historians have treated caste denoting 'fragmentation' at social level as the hallmark of Indian culture.

Such monolithic interpretations by imperialist writers – though dominant and inspiring in administrative circles – were not shared by all and sundry. For example, E.W. Hopkins underlined the historical value of epics and highlighted the material speculation, parallel to the religious one in Indian tradition. T.W. Rhys Davids's discovery of existence of republics besides monarchy in ancient India in his *Buddhist India* (1903) marked an interpretative change in ancient Indian political studies. Besides, several archaeological findings by James Princep, Alexander Cunningham and many others provided the authentic source material to relook at India's past.

Nationalist Historiography

The emergence of nationalist historiography in the second half of the 19th century was primarily an Indian response to the Europeans' verdict on India's past. Revelation of glorious past by Max Müller like indologists and some archaeological discoveries reminded Indians of their forgotten history. Thus imperialist historiography itself, though inadvertently, facilitated the genesis of nationalist historiography. But it was the national movement that provided not only inner strength but also a definite shape and direction to nationalist historiography. R.S. Sharma draws a parallel between the trends of nationalist movement and its impact on history writing. Just as there were two phases: moderate and extremist in the growth of the nationalist movement; so was the case with the development of nationalist historiography.[27]

In the first phase of nationalist movement, the main demand from the Indian National Congress forum was to curtail the autocratic power of viceroy, tax reforms and increase in the rights of Indians in councils. Hence in 1887, R.C. Dutt in his article 'Civilisation in the Brahamana Period' tried to show that in ancient times the king did justice to all.[28] Purnendu Narayan Singh followed the same path and argued that the system of government in ancient India was 'limited monarchy'. Both of them countered the statement of Sir Auckland Colvin that the British have taught for the first time that the aim of rule is welfare of the people. During the last three decades of the 19th century, Bhagwan Lal Indraji, R.G. Bhandarkar, R.L. Mitra were important historians who with their researches tried to establish a brightful past of India.

The year of 1905 was turning point as it marks the beginning of the extremist phase of Indian national movement. The autocratic policies of Lord Curzon (1899–1905), especially the partition of Bengal, influenced the course of nationalist politics as well as historiography. Extremist leaders – mainly the triumvirate Lal, Bal, Pal – called for *'Swaraj'*, and also endorsed the use of force and violence to uproot British rule. At this point of time, the discovery of Kautilya's *Arthasastra* in 1905 and its publication by Shamashastri in 1909 proved to be the strongest weapon to energize Indian intelligentsia. Consequently the history-writing too became eloquent, sharp and somewhat attacking in nature, as reflected in writings of scholars like K.P. Jayaswal, D.R. Bhandarkar, B.K. Sirkar, N.N. Law, R.C. Majumdar and others.

It is to K.P. Jayaswal that nationalist historiography owes its greatest work on ancient Indian polity. His articles contributed to *Modern Review* (A monthly journal published by R. Chatterji from Calcutta) between 1912 and 1915 – which appeared later in the form of his well-known book *Hindu Polity* in 1924 – were really watershed development in the growth of nationalist historiography.

Jayaswal propounded that democratic elements could be traced in the ancient Indian polity in the working of Vedic assemblies. The procedure employed to arrive at decisions in such assemblies were akin to modern days of parliamentary functioning. If a matter entailed a division in the opinion of members, speeches were made and the procedure of majority was observed.[29]

Besides monarchy, republics were also present in ancient India. He tried to prove that anncient Hindu political system was partly of republics of Athenian type and partly of the constitutional monarchy such as that of Great Britain. Constitutionalism or the supremacy of law was presumed by the nationalists as an important feature of ancient Indian polity. There was all powerful law, the common law of Hindus which is declared again and again to be above the king and as the king of kings.[30] Jayaswal also pointed out that taxes were fixed by law and the scales had been embodied in the sacred common law.[31] Judiciary always remained separate from the executive. The state was a trust which was created for the prosperity of the people.[32]

With these conclusions, Jayaswal challenged the imperialistic notions regarding the polity and law of Ancient India such as Oriental Despotism, absence of rule of law, etc. He also presented the first solid ideological case for complete independence and a republican form of government in India.[33]

The lead given by Jayaswal was followed by a number of scholars with varied field of research. R.C. Majumdar opposed the imperialistic proposition that Indian society was divided into watertight compartments by caste system. He asserted that the spirit of cooperation was a marked feature in ancient India and religion did not engross the whole or even an undue proportion of public attention.[34]

The third phase of national movement, which began with the advent of Mahatma Gandhi, had its own bearings on the history-writing. Besides ethical values of truth and non-violence, Gandhi took great interest in the upliftment of depressed class like Dalits and women and in maintaining communal harmony in the country. Critical analysis and ever-eagerness to rectify drawbacks of our society were the hallmark of Gandhian thought. Spread of Marxist ideology especially after the formation of Communist Party of India (CPI) in 1925 and ongoing social reform movements played a significant role in shaping the historical trends of Gandhian era. J.L. Nehru, B.R. Ambedkar, P.V. Kane, U.N. Ghoshal, Beni Prasad,

R.K. Mookerji are some of the important historians of this phase.

Nehru as a historian, apart from being a great political figure, believed that unlike today's reality, it was Asia which dominated over Europe in ancient period in the field of valour and wisdom.[35] But Nehru was not guided by intense nationalism, rather by scientific temperament, rationality and socialism which produced dispassionate and critical analysis of Indian history in his writings.

B.R. Ambedkar took doubt and inquiry as the basis of any form of knowledge including the historical one. He asserted that of all the ills afflicting our society the caste-system with the notion of untouchability as its necessary fall out was the most debilitating one. Accepting fellow-feeling or fraternity as the basis of democracy, he claimed that democracy could never grow in India because Hindu religion does not teach fraternity.[36] Though Nehru and Ambedakar were not professional historians but their ideologies and analysis of the past influenced generations of historians. Later Beni Prasad too held up many of Ambedakar's view and admitted that caste, apart from the fact that it rules out democracy, also strikes at the root of individuality.[37]

U.N. Ghoshal utilized the Buddhist canons as well to analyze polity and laws of ancient India. He rejected the imperialist notion of all-pervading spirituality and emphasized that three elements – spirituality, intellectuality and vitality, which formed the Indian genius, have shaped the growth of ancient social and political theories.[38]

A.S. Altekar applied the anthropological findings in historical studies and came out with a conclusion that the institution of joint family gradually led to the evolution of kingship.[39] P.V. Kane was against the tendency to compare ancient institutions of India with modern European concepts. On the basis of his erudite studies of the *Dharmsastras*, he declared that the vast literature on politics is contained in Sanskrit and Pali works which have often been overlooked by Europeans.[40]

After the perusal of the views of the important nationalist historian, now it becomes clear that with the passage of time and perspective, the temper and tenor of nationalist historiography also changed. Here it would also not be improper to point out certain drawbacks which crept into nationalist historiography covering a long period.

The nationalist historians concerned themselves with those ideas which were necessary to nationalist polemics. They questioned individual items of historical interpretations, rather than the validity of a (imperialist) theory as a total pattern of interpretations.[41] Far from challenging the theory of Aryan race and periodization of Indian history on religious grounds, they somehow approved them. By giving undue focus on and in adoring ancient Indian Hindu institutions, nationalist historians tended to, though unwittingly, antagonize the Muslims. They chose their research topic from ancient India, and this trend not only overlooked the medieval achievements but also contributed to suitable atmosphere for the success of 'Divide and Rule policy' by British. R.S. Sharma notes that nationalist historians must have focused on the point that it was not India alone where religion influenced human activity. Instead many scholars fought shy of religious aspects of ancient Indian polity.[42] Another important characteristic of nationalist historiography which often had negative fall out, as Romila Thapar puts it, was the fact that cultural revival became entangled with religious revival, ignoring the socio-political terms of nationalism.[43]

In spite of these limitations, nobody can deny the immense contributions of nationalist historians to history-writing in the country. New discoveries, decipherments of inscriptions, translations and publications of ancient texts were made at larger level during the period. The historians countered the imperialist notions and pronounced many bold hypotheses, which later served as the foundation of further research. Besides, they placed an ideological weapon in the hands of Indian nationalists, struggling for self-government and freedom and filled the people with great self-confidence. As many European historians were serving both imperialistic and academic purposes, similarly historians of this school were guided not only by scholarly interests but also by nationalist politics. This explains well many of drawbacks found in nationalist historiography.

Marxist Historiography

The emergence of Marxism in the middle of nineteenth century was an epoch-making event, not only for the global politics but for historiography as well. It changed the thought-pattern fundamentally and initiated new dimensions, patterns, models and ideals of approaching the past. Marx's theory regarding history is called 'Historical Materialism', which is economic interpretations of history, employing his core principle, i.e., Dialectic Materialism. Marx believes that the course of history is dialectic and imminent. It proceeds ahead because of the conflict between the exploitating class (bourgeoisie) and exploited people (proletariats). So, all history is the story of class struggle.

The theory of historical materialism asserts that economic or material aspect of social life is 'basic structure' on which all other social values and institutions called 'super-structure' such as state, religion and morality ideologies are built. The change in 'basic structure' leads to the change in superstructure. Since mode of production constitutes the greater part of 'basic structure', so it determines the course of history. It is called 'economic determinism'. Relying on various modes of production, Marx divided history into six phases or ages.

1. Primitive communism
2. Slavery
3. Feudalism
4. Capitalism
5. Socialism
6. Communism

So the ultimate goal of history is to establish the communist society which would be a stateless, classless and exploitation-less stage. People will work according to their capacity and would be paid according to their needs. There are many other Marxist concepts such a^ theories of revolution, surplus value, private property, false consciousness, etc., which have influenced the historical interpretations deeply.

Application of Marxist perception in Indian history-writing began with Marx himself. In the two letters published in 1853 in New York's *Daily Tribune*, Marx asserted that the Indian past conformed by and large to what he called the 'Asiatic Mode of Production' characterized by a static society (unchanging East) and absence of private property in land, self-sufficient villages and a state control over the irrigation system. Although he and Engels recognized deviations from this pattern and argued that historical stagnancy in India was broken by the coming of British colonialism. But this view of Indian past was not supported by even the Marxist historian in general. S.A. Dange, D.D. Kosambi, N.N. Bose and later R.S. Sharma, Romila Thapar, D.N. Jha among many others strengthened and enriched the Marxist history-writing of ancient India.

The credit to set the tone and temper of Marxist historiography in India goes to D.D. Kosambi. A mathematician by profession, Kosambi evolved a paradigm shift in historiography by defining history as 'the presentation, in chronological order of successive developments in the means and relations of production'.[44] For D.D. Kosambi, the more important question is not who was king or whether the given region had a king, but whether people used a plough, light or heavy, at the time.[45] Applying, the tool of historical materialism, he says that dynastic changes may be studied in as so far they indicate powerful changes in the productive basis.[46] He, applying his knowledge of Sanskrit and etymological analysis, reconstructed the social background of ancient India, particularly of Vedic period, and his mathematical aptitude helped him analysing Indian numismatics, mainly punch-marked coins. His major contribution lies in adopting a comparative and inter-disciplinary method, relating text to its context, interpretation of myths and feudalist structure in Indian history, etc.

Kosambi maintained that the basic factor of transition from tribe to caste owing to introduction of plough culture is one of the clues to an understanding of the Indian past.[47] But Kosambi never accepted the Marxist model *in toto*; rather, he applied its method of analysis. As he stated that Marxism was not being 'proved' or justified, but simply being used as a tool of professional investigation.[48]

R.S. Ṣharma, a front-rank historian of post-independent India, has studied various aspects of ancient India history with the Marxist method of research. In addition to his studies on socio-economic history of Early India, he has analysed the origin and nature of state, administrative structure and politico-legal concepts of ancient India in his *Aspects of Political Ideas and Institutions in Ancient India* (1968). In this respect, he has critically examined the imperialist and nationalist historiography of ancient Indian polity and law, and proposed its interpretation in the light of socio-economic process.

R.S. Sharma maintains that the theory of *Saptanga* state as described in *Arthasastra* seems resembling with that of Engels. The public officials, public power and taxes may be compared to *Arthsastra*'s *amatyas, danda* and *Kosa*.[49] He believes that the *Krta* (golden) age described in law books, was the period of stateless society or the state of nature. It disappeared due to the emergence of institutions of private property, family and *Varna*, paving the way for the origin of state.[50] Further, he categorically observes: 'In my opinion the origin and growth of the taxation system determines the rise and development of the state.'[51]

For R.S. Sharma, *Mauryan* polity represented the state of centralised bureaucracy followed by divinity and decentralization in the Post-Mauryan phase. He described the Gupta state-system as the 'proto-feudal' polity and analysed it in the light of increasing practice of land grants. His *Material Culture and Social Formations in Ancient India* (1983) runs strictly along Marxist lines of historical analysis and interpretation. Prof. Sharma, by his well-researched publications such as *Shudras in Ancient India* (1958), *Indian Feudalism* (1966), and *Urban Decay in India* (1987) enriched new horizons of ancient Indian studies and inspired many others to undertake similar pursuits.

Romila Thapar has contributed immensely in the development of Marxist historiography of ancient India. In her first scholarly publication, *Ashoka and Decline of the Mauryas* (1963), she reinterpreted Asokan *Dhamma* as a political and social necessity of the age rather than the moral effulgence of an idealistic monarch. Prof. Thapar echoes historical materialism in her more popular book *History of India* (1966), while asserting that 'changes in political pattern are inextricably entwined in changes in the economic structure and these, in turn, have a bearing on the social relationships'.[52] In her *Ancient Indian Social History* (1978), she analyses the social and legal life in early India. She observes that the Hindu tradition was generally discriminatory in law, caste-ridden and inegalitarian in social relations ... while the heterodox tradition (Jainism and Buddhism) emphasized the equality of human beings, the equality of all before law and disapproved of slavery.[53] *From Lineage to State* (1984) is a perceptive analysis of the process of state formation in early India. Thapar traces the origin of the state system in the Ganga Valley to the transition from lineage mode of production to a peasant economy of private holdings and increasing urbanization. She has explained the references to origin of state, as found in *Santi Parva* of *Mahabharata*, with Marxist perception. In her view, the elimination of *Nishad* and installation of *Prithu* must be interpreted as the victory of land agriculture over nomadic life.[54] In *Ideology and Interpretation of Early Indian History* (The first essay in *Cultural Past*, 2004), Thapar questioned two pervading stereotypes prorogated by Westerners: the theory of the Aryan race and the notion of Oriental Despotism. Here, her assertion is based on the bunch of new evidences supplied by archaeology, linguistics and social anthropology.

From the above survey of three major schools of Indian historiography, it becomes obvious that ancient Indian studies in general are enriched highly. The Indologists initiated modern study of India's past which later was strengthened by Utilitarian and Romanticist historians. But since their interpretations more or less followed imperialistic perceptions, so they were challenged by Indian historians generally called 'nationalists'. Nationalist historians, in their zeal to refute their imperialist counterparts, idealized the ancient Indian achievements but often overlooked the socio-economic conflicts apparently present in the same past. Marxist historians highlighted this aspect greatly and tried to look at ancient India and its legal system more realistically; but their too much emphasis on materialistic approach led them to sideline some important aspects of ancient Indian religion, philosophy and culture.

Post-modern Paradigms

In the post-independent period imperialist versus nationalist debate lost its charm and the Marxists too began to be guided by new discourses namely, social justice, economic rebuilding, secular politics, etc. But the biggest factor which influenced the course of post-independent Indian historiography is post-modernism. Post-modernism, an intellectual movement of post-colonial world, attacked the core belief of modernity such as identity, unity, authority, certainty, etc., and instead popularized difference, plurality, textuality, skepticism. It is marked by the total loss of faith in Enlightenment scientific rationality and ideas of progress, which received a traumatic shock in the two World Wars.

Post-modernist thinkers namely, Jean Francois Lyotard (*The Post Modern Condition*, 1979), rejected the superiority complex of European white culture calling it meta-narrative and advocated for the freedom and significance of every group and society equally. Jacques Derrida's 'Deconstructionism' arguing for the various different meanings of a text persuaded historians to look more closely at historical documents in new ways.

In such an atmosphere Europeans interest in Indology got renewed with new interpretive models. They started studying India's past with more evidence-based, corroborative and comparative method, and often deviated from earlier imperialist stereotypes. The French Indologist Robert Lingat studied the different phases of Hindu law in his *Classical Law of India* (translated and published in 1973) and admitted that with the commentaries and digests, a true juridical science began in India.[55]

British scholar J.D.M. Derrett produced two major works: ***Religion, Law and State in India*** (1968) and *Essays in Classical and Modern Hindu Law* (1977). He has rightly been called the

Maharshi on the bank of Thames for his almost unbiased and sensitive studies of the *Dharmasastras*. Derrett's successor W.F. Menski analysed the growth-story of Hindu law from Vedic period to the age of globalization with typical post-modernist approach in his *Hindu Law: Beyond Tradition and Modernity* (2003). Donald R. Davis in his recently published book *The Spirit of Hindu Law* (2011) argues that ancient India envisaged the 'rule of lawful' rather than 'rule of law' and therefore avoided the problems arising from the total depersonalization of legal system.[56]

All these Indologists and historians reflect a paradigm shift in western approaches to Indian past in general and its legal aspect in particular. Indeed, history-writing is a dynamic process and a continuous kind of human activity. It is very much vulnerable to historian's own intellectual conviction and contemporary socio-political or economic structure. This is why we come across different schools of historiography: imperialist, nationalist, Marxist and recently post-modernist which have viewed the past in their own way. Irrespective of their merits and demerits, which is almost inherent in the nature of historiography, all of them have enriched profusely our understanding of ancient India in general and it's legal scenario in particular.

Notes

1. Varma, Lal Bahadur, *Understanding History*, p. 22.
2. Butterfield, Herbert, *'Historiography.', in Dictionary of History of Ideas*, Vol. 2, p. 464.
3. Ernest John, Knapton, quoted in E. Sreedharan's *A Textbook of Historiography* (500 BC to AD 2000), p. 107.
4. Collingwood, R.G., *The Idea of History*, p. 86–87.
5. Ali, B. Sheik, *History: Its Theory and Method*, p. 227.
6. *Blackwell Dictionary of Historians* quoted in E. Sreedharan's op. cit., p. 188.
7. Ranke, Quoted in E.H. Carr's, *What is History*? p. 5.

8. Marwick, quoted in E. Sreedharan's, op. cit., p. 193.
9. The details are described in the section of Marxist historiography.
10. Quoted in E.H., Carr, op. cit., p. 20–21.
11. Collingwood, R.G., op. cit., p. 215.
12. Hastings quoted in J.P. Marshall's *British Discovery of Hindustan*, p. 189.
13. Thapar, Romila, *Cultural Past, Essays in Early Indian History*, p. 4.
14. Spear, P. *Oxford History*, p. 513
15. Winternitz, M., *A History of Indian Literature*, p. 14.
16. Müller, Max, *A History of Sanskrit Literature*, p. xvii.
17. Thapar, Romila, op. cit., p. 5.
18. Kejariwal, O.P., *Asiatic Society of Bengal*, p. 228.
19. Mill, James, *The History of British India*, p. 167–168.
20. Ibid., p. 155.
21. Quoted in Beni Prasad's, *The State in Ancient India*, p. 498.
22. Mill, James, op. cit., p. 175.
23. Elphinstone, M., *The History of India*, p. 61.
24. Ibid., p. 33.
25. Smith, Vincent, *Early History of India*, p. 30.
27. Lorenzen, D., *Imperialism and the Historiography of Ancient India*, published in *India: History and Thought, Essays in Honor of A.L. Basham*, editedby S.N. Mukhaejee, p. 86.
28. Sharma, R.S., *Aspects of Political Ideas and Institutions in Ancient India*, p. 3.
29. *Calcutta Review*, xxxv (1887) quoted by R.S. Sharma, ibid., p. 3.
30. Jayaswal, K.P., *Hindu Polity*, p. 91.
31. Ibid., p. 310.
32. Ibid. p. 319.
33. Ibid., p. 342.
34. Sharma, R.S., op. cit., p. 5.

35. Majumdar, R.C., *Corporate Life in Ancient India*, p. 1–2.
36. Nehru, J.L., *Glimpses of World History*, p. 9–10.
37. Ambedkar, B.R., *Writings and Speeches*, Vol. IV, p. 283.
38. Prasad, Beni, *The State in Ancient India*, p. 11.
39. Ghashal, U.N., *A History of Indian Political Ideas*, p. 9.
40. Altekar, A.S., *State and Government in Ancient India*, p. 35.
41. Kane, P.V., *History of Dharmasastra*, Vol. III, p. 15.
42. Thapar, Romila, op. cit., p. 9.
43. Sharma, R.S., op. cit., p. 12.
44. Thapar, Romila, *The Past and Prejudices*, p. 12.
45. Kosambi, D.D., *An Introduction to the study of Indian History*, 1956, Bombay, p. 1.
46. Ibid., pp. 12–13.
47. Ibid., p. 13.
48. Ibid., p. 24.
51. Ibid., p. 55.
52. Ibid., p. 198.
53. Thapar, Romila, *History of India*, Vol. 1, p. 22.
53. ——. 'Society and Law in the Hindu and Buddhist traditions', in Ancient Indian Social History, p. 34.
54. ——. *From Lineage to State*, pp. 117–18.
55. Lingatm, Robert. *The Classical Law of India*, p. 143.
56. Davis, Donald R., *The Spirit of Hindu Law*, Cambridge University Press, Book Review, Published in *The Hindu*, New Delhi Edition, 31 May 2011.

2

The Notion of Law in Ancient India

Reflections from Modern Historians

In modern theory of jurisprudence, law is considered the set of prescriptive rules, framed by a sovereign state for its citizen. But in ancient Indian context, we see a highly inclusive definition of law wherein cosmic laws (*rit*), social and moral duty (often termed as *dharma*), religious ceremonies, customary rules, along with administrative regulations, all constituted the body of law. This open-ended concept of law caused difficulties not only in the clear classification of laws (as into civil and criminal) but also in determining the exact source and reformer of law. State and judiciary are often the executive bodies to carry out laws framed by law-givers, who were mainly Brahminis, called *Dharmasastrakara*. But the law-givers too were not unanimous on every issue and differed very often in relation to their time and space.

Beside this ramified nature of law, historians' own intellectual conviction and their guiding interests (such as imperialism or nationalism) have led to the emergence of innumerable interpretations of the concept of law in ancient India. Europeans initiated the study of ancient Indian law in late 18th century to serve their scholarly interests, coupled with imperialistic/administrative requirements as described in the first chapter. But soon they were followed by Indian historians, termed as 'nationalist' who confronted many of imperialist assumptions about ancient Indian law. Distinct from these two, the Marxist historians tried to look at the notion of law in relation to socio-economic process in ancient India. Consequently, the different aspects of ancient Indian legal concept such as nature, kinds, sources and limitations of laws, came to be studied in greater detail.

The first concrete step in the direction of understanding the concept of ancient Indian law was undertaken by Warren Hastings (1772–85). He asked some Brahmans who were well versed in Sanskrit and law to compile a book based on Indian law books. This book containing important information about laws regarding family, marriage, property, inheritance, etc., was entitled *Vivadarnavasetu*. Its English translation by Nathenial Brassey appeared with the title *A Code of Gentoo Law.* Sir William Jones, who is regarded as the father of British Indology, translated the *Manusmriti* in 1794 with the title *Institutes of Hindu Law* or the *Ordinances of Manu.* However the real stimulus to the study of ancient Indian law was given by H.T. Colebrooke, who succeeded Jones as the chief of Asiatic Society of Bengal. He was one of those few early scholars who knew Hindu law and Sanskrit well. Colebrooke's two treatises, *The Hindu Law of Inheritance* and *A Digest of Hindu Law on Contracts and Successions*, proved to be the standard books for later studies and researches.

Jones and Colebrooke translated and studied the laws books of ancient Indian but the interpretative direction of the early historiography of the subject was established by the typical imperialist historians like James Mill. Mill in his famous book *The History of British India* (1820) devoted a full chapter to ancient Indian law entitled 'The Laws of Hindus'. This chapter deals with the concept of Hindu law, its classification, and laws pertaining to inheritance, crime, punishment, adultery, witness, judiciary, etc.

Mill in his observation finds that Hindus have treated un-matching subjects of laws such as: ceremonies of religion, rules and practice of education, customs of domestic life, and rules of governments of war and negotiation and jurisprudence in the same style. In his view, this conjunction of dissimilar subjects made the important distinction between obligations of state or magistrate and sanctions of morality and self-interest disappear. Mill regards this disappearance of difference as a deliberate way to extend the coercion, and the authority of magistrate over the greater part of human life and to leave men no liberty even in their private and ordinary transactions.[1]

Mill, quoting the *Institutes of Manu*, wherein divisions of law are eighteen, criticizes vehemently the arrangement and classification of the matter of law by Hindus. He asserts,

> 'It is not easy to conceive a *more rude* and defective attempt at classification of laws, than what is here presented. The most essential and obvious distinctions are neglected and confounded. Though no arrangement would appear more natural, and more likely to strike even an uncultivated mind, than the division of laws into civil and penal, we find them mixed and blended together in the code of Hindus'.[2]

Mill's adherence to this school of utilitarianism and the erstwhile prevailing ideas of *laissez faire*, etc., are evident in his interpretation of ancient Indian history in general and Hindu law in particular. For example, he condemns Manu for authorizing the king to regulate the sale and purchase of all marketable things. In his words: 'The regulation which fixes the prices of things instead of leaving it to the natural and beneficent laws of competition, conveys not a high idea of the knowledge of the Hindus'.[3]

According to Mill, 'Completeness' and 'Exactness' are the two constituents of the body of law.[4] 'Completeness' means including everything necessary and 'exactness' stands for exclusion of all extraneous matters. With these parameters, Mill evaluates the Hindu law and sees several flaws in it, such as, lack of accurate definition, omission of many parts of law, vague and contradictory style.

Relying on such interpretations, Mill firmly held the notion that before the coming of Britishers, Indians were unaware of a rational and scientific juridical system. Such an interpretation of Indian past, feels Romila Thapar, 'came in a very handy to British administration since he maintained that legislation could change a society. This was in a sense a sanction to the British administration to legislate change in its own interests'.[5]

Among the early British juridical writers, perhaps the most important name is that of Sir Henry Sumner Maine (1822–88). Maine belonged to the school of Historical Jurisprudence or Legal Evolutionism which believed that the laws are not static things but subject to change in accordance with historical process of social change. He was initiated towards studying the law of India by James Mill and thus imbibed to a large extent the views and notions of his mentor. His most famous work *Ancient law*, followed by *The Effects of Observation of India on Modern Europeans Thoughts (1875)*, *Dissertations on Early law and Custom (1883)* reflected the general tone of imperialist historiography.

Maine believes that Indian legal system was stagnant, unpractical and incomplete and put off on a docile public by interested compilers who were priests.[6] The caste system and women under 'perpetual tutelage' are cited by Maine as instances of stagnation. He also sees the overbearing influence of religious class in formulation of laws in Eastern world. He says, 'The religious oligarchies of Asia, either for their own guidance, or for the relief of their memory, or for the instruction of their disciples, seem in all cases to have ultimately embodied their legal learning in a code'.[7] He adds, 'The Hindoo Code called *The Laws of Manu* does not, as a whole, represent a set of rules ever actually administered in Hindostan. It is in great part, an ideal picture of that which, in the view of the Brahmins, *ought* to be the law.'[8]

Maine holds the notion that religion pervaded the sphere of law extremely. He writes very candidly, 'Among the Hindoos, the religious element in law has acquired a complete predominance. Family sacrifices have become the keystone of all the Laws of Persons and much of the Laws of Things. They have even received a monstrous extension.'[9]

Being a scholar of Roman and British legal history, Maine had the advantage of comparing and contrasting the Indian law and legal system with its European counterparts. In his words,

> 'Ethnology shows us that the Romans and the Hindoos sprang from the same original stock, and there is indeed a striking

resemblance between what appear to have been their original customs. Even now, Hindoo jurisprudence has a substratum of forethought and sound judgment, but irrational imitation has engrafted in it an immense apparatus of cruel absurdities. From these corruptions the Romans were protected by their code.'[10]

Despite such presumptions, Maine made a comprehensive study of ancient Indian law and concluded that it had some peculiarities and must not be forced to fit English legal terms and concepts. It seems as if imperialist interests and his own belief in legal evolutionism have intermingled, often in favour of former, in his study of ancient Indian law.

But the credit to establish the utility of vast body of the *Dharmasastra* literature to understand the law goes to Indologists like G. Buhler, J. Jolly and A.B. Keith. These scholars were learned both in Sanskrit and law, and thus had the advantage of probing original Indian sources and analysing their legal significance. German scholar Jolly's *Hindu Law and Custom* is an important book for its in-depth and thorough analysis which according to Lallanji Gopal, is the first authentic study of *Dharmasastra*.[11]

Jolly has translated and published many ancient Indian legal texts such as, *Narad* and *Brihaspati Smritis*, named *The Minor Law-Books* (First published in 1889). In his introduction to the translation of *Narad Smriti,* he highlighted the connection between Manu and Narad. In his view, Narad developed many theories whose germs may be traced to the *Code of Manu*, his (Narad's) judicial theories show an infinitely advanced stage of development as compared to Manu's.[12] It is a matter of fact that in several cases, doctrines, propounded by Narad, are opposed to and cannot be viewed in the light of developments from the teachings of Manu. For example, Narad supports the practice of *Niyoga,* remarriage of widows, and legalizes gambling in public-houses and heir-ship of even youngest qualified son. These instances are taken by Jolly to infer that *Narard Smriti* is the only Smriti, in which law is treated by itself, without any reference to rules of penance and other religious subjects, and it throws a new and an important light on the political and social institutions of ancient India at the time of its composition.[13]

But Jolly too, seems to uphold the imperialist notion regarding religious impact on the concept of law. He opined that the religious thoughts have shaped the social history of India and the law is an integral part of religion and custom.[14] G. Buhler translated and published *Manu Smriti* in the 25th Vol. of S.B.E. series. As a variation from the alleged notion that ancient India did not witness the growth of law, Buhler sees the existence of 'Special Law School'. He, while commenting on the nature of such schools observes, 'These law schools were independent of any particular *sakha* of the *veda*, and supplanted the *vedic charanas* as far as the teaching of the sacred law is concerned.'[15] He tries to explain the process through which these law schools emerged and says, 'Vedic schools first systematized and cultivated the six sciences such as 'school of law', which restricted the range of their teaching, taught their curriculum thoroughly and intelligently came into existence.'[16] Such sensitive studies by Buhler can well be understood in the light of a somewhat different account of Indian past given by Indologists. But, unfortunately, it was the imperialist vision that dominated Western mind. Some other prominent names who contributed immensely towards the study of law in ancient India include Whitley Stokes, J. Meyer, A.D. Diamond, Sir John Miles, Duncan Forbes, etc.

But the imperialist assumptions regarding the law of ancient India did not go unopposed. By the end of 19th century, nationalist historians began to study the original texts in Sanskrit, and confronted various historical judgments of Europeans. Most of these nationalist historians emphasized upon the fact that society, polity and law were at an advanced stage in ancient India. K.P. Jayaswal in his well-known book *Hindu Polity* (1924) rejected most of the imperialist perceptions such as 'despotic government' and 'absence of rule of law' in ancient India. He proposed that Hindu law was above the king and it had been often described as the 'King of Kings'. In his words, 'even in the palmiest days of Hindu Monarchy ... the King was not placed above the law. He could pass only regulatory laws but not the substantive ones'.[17] Jayaswal treated the *Dharma-sastra,* as a corpus of law similar to those found in English and Roman traditions and also as a proof that the Indians were capable of administering law to themselves thus rendering the Europeans' superfluous.

Some of the important works which shaped the course of nationalist historiography pertaining to the notion of law are: *The General Principles of Hindu Jurisprudence* (1918) by P.N. Sen; *Principles of Hindu Law* (first edtion, 1912) by Dinshah F. Mulla; *Manu and Yagyavalkya* (1930) by K.P. Jayswal; *History of Dharmasastra,* (Vols. I–III, 1930–46) by P.V. Kane; *Rajdharma* (1941); by K.V. Rangaswamy Aiyangar; *Hindu law and its Sources,* (1933) by G.N. Jha.

K.V.R. Aiyangar, in line of K.P. Jayswal, observes that ancient India did witness the rule of law. Regarding the power of king he says: 'He (king) cannot make a new law, royal edict is merely declamatory, and not innovative.'[18] Prevalence of positive laws and even the concept of law depicting the will of community in ancient India were highlighted by some nationalist scholars. P.N. Banerjee distinguishes between the two classes of laws (i) the laws of rituals or moral laws and (ii) positive laws. Sanction for the first kind was religious or social, and for the second, political.[19] Dikshitar talks of the existence of democratic elements in the polity of ancient India. He says 'the sanction of law has the common will as the basis and so long this idea of the common will underlies these legal principles, the law operates satisfactorily to all, whether you call it law, morality or by any other name. This common will is nothing but the expression of healthy public opinion which is a feature of ancient Indian democracy'.[20]

Nationalist historians also countered the notion of stagnant law in ancient India which was proposed by imperialists, and often by Marxists, in the light of 'unchanging East'. Nationalists assert that though the laws considered sacred and eternal, they were also influenced by accepted customs and local usages. K.P. Jayswal extracting the lines from *Sukraniti* affirms that the Hindus had developed a particular method of legal reforms.[21] In his view, the traditional law was altered by direct legislation, interpretation and also by new treatises. Some of the methods employed by the writers and commentators of *Smritis* were the theories of *Kali-Varjya* (acts forbidden in the Kali-age) and '*apad-dharma*' (acts performed in emergency which are not in conformity to the caste of the performer but are treated as valid). The theory of *Kali-Varjya*, thinks Kane, furnishes peremptory argument against the still widespread prejudice of the 'unchanging East'.[22]

U.N. Ghoshal produced extensive as well as intensive study of ancient Indian concepts of polity and law from Vedic period to 13th century AD, in his *A History of Indian Political Ideas* (originally published in 1923). He has surveyed not only the legal texts of Brahamanical and Buddhist traditions but also the Tamil literature and epigraphic materials. In the first chapter *General Introduction* of his book, Ghoshal rejected many imperialist criticism regarding ancient Indian political ideas. In his view, religion never exercised an exclusive hold on the Indian mind as to preclude it from conceiving political theories and besides, traditional Indian list of sciences always contained some secular branches of knowledge, namely politics and economics.[23]

Ghoshal assesses the Willoughby's criticism that stresses on the alleged dogmatic belief of Indians in the Divine Creation and ordering of world in two aspects: social and political. He accepts that Vedic dogmas of Divine Creation of the social order formed basis to some extent, but there was always scope for relevant modifications. In his words, 'while the *Smritis* hold the canon to be the primary source of the law of the social order, they lay down principles for adjusting this law to the needs and capacities as well as sentiments of the people. What is more, they expressly declare more than once that the ultimate test of the law of the social order is the judgment of the cultured and enlightened people.'[24] In the political field, the branch of state law, says Ghoshal, while the early Smritis conceive the canon and custom to be its twofold source, Kautilya in his great work on the technical science of polity adds two other sources, namely, the current law (*Arthasastra)* and reasoning, which in the event of conflict with canon, will prevail'.[25]

Ghoshal observes that Manu and Yajnvalkya and their successors were evidently under the influence of Kautilaya, stressing on reasoning. Accordingly, they have credited the king's executive edict with the force of law. He remarks: 'It is perhaps permissible to find in these successive stages of development of the Indian concept of State law a distant parallel to the stages of Ancient Roman law marked by the *responsa prudenta*, the *aequitas* and the *lex*.'[26]

It is noticeable that nationalist historians, in order to challenge their imperialist counterparts not only appreciated the concept of ancient Indian law, but also projected it as superior to any other contemporary systems of law. In this respect P.N. Sen highlighted many features of 'excellence' of Hindu jurisprudence such as: comprehensiveness of Hindu law, loftiness of ideals, logical consistency, reasonableness, regard for the interest of the community and practical insight.[27]

Here, the basis of divinity of law which became the general voice of nationalist writers needs to be mentioned. Since, *Sruti* or Vedas which are the first and primary source of law are not written by anybody but were heard by *Rishis* or were revealed to them, so emerged the concept of Divine Hindu law. This element of divinity is viewed by nationalist scholars as the supremacy of law; because it could not be altered by anyone including the king. But as an innate contradiction, this feature also leads to the perception of stagnant law as emphasized by imperialist historians.

The erudite work of P.V. Kane's *History of Dharmasastra* is perhaps the most comprehensive study on the concept of law and legal institutions in ancient India. He makes a critical assessment of various *Dharmasastras*, and endeavours to explain the contradictions found there in by taking into account the developments of modern historiography. He compares the ancient Indian legal traditions with its European counterparts and observes that in ancient India, law was not immutable, stagnant and dogmatic. As cited above, he believes that in accordance with the custom and usage, ancient Indian law was subject to change.

In volume III of *History of Dharmasastra*, Kane discusses in detail *Rajadharma* (duties of the king) *Vyavahara* (dispute, a law suit) and *Sadachara* (actions of good people). He assumes that authors of *Smritis* believed that there was a golden age or era of perfect divinity, later ages saw the advent of sinful promptings and therefore, regulations of life by the learned and king came into vogue.[28] These diametrically opposite views: state of perfection in the divine past and anarchy of the later period contained in the same works such as *Manu* and *Mahabharata* probably owe their origin to the desire of the writers to make the common people submit to the absolute rule of kings. A state of anarchy is visualized in a few works only for the purpose of glorifying the great usefulness of the institution of the kingship.[29] *Dharma*, as Kane puts it, took the place of the very ancient conception of *Rita* which in the *Rig Veda* denotes the superior transcendental law or the cosmic order by which the universe and even the gods are governed, and which intimately is connected with the sacrifice.[30]

Kane takes '*Vyavahara*' to mean 'lawsuit' or dispute in a court and legal procedure. The eighteen '*Vyavaharpadas* include both civil and criminal law. Kane observes 'the enumeration of *Vyavaharapadas,* is very ancient and authoritative; but there is hardly any scientific principle of classification underlying them.[31] It is noticeable that James Mill earlier had claimed that in the divisions of Hindu law no principle of arrangement and classification can be traced.[32] However, Kane gives a justification to some of Mill's assertions about Hindu law such as, conjunction of dissimilar subjects and treatment of un-matching chapters in the same style. He says that though a distinction was made between civil and criminal disputes among the 18 titles of law, it appears that the set of rules and procedure in both were the same, the same courts tried both the kinds of disputes and not as in modern times.[33] In Kane's opinion this sameness explains the mix up of civil and criminal laws.

In Kane's support, it can be pointed out that nowadays in India, civil matters are handled by District Judge (D.J.), Additional D.J., Civil Judge (Sr. and Jr.), whereas for criminal matters, separate session courts are provided.[34] It is improper to search similar systems in the distant past. Kane adds, 'Ancient system cannot be expected to present such a classification ... They (*Smrit*-writers) more or less deal with most of the subjects brought out in modern classifications but not in an orderly manner. They also divided laws into substantive and adjective or procedural. The *Vyavaharapadas* correspondence to the former and rules about procedure, the appointment of judges, evidence and limitations are adjective laws.[35]

Kane upholds the general point that along with *Sruti* and *Smriti*, customs were also among the chief sources of law in ancient India. In case of conflict between, *Sruti Smriti* and *achara* (custom), it was a general principle that the preceding one will replace the succeeding one. But for Kane, the conflict of *Smritis* among themselves presents greater difficulties which were due to the changing society and new requirements accordingly.[36] Apart from above aspects of the notion of law, Kane has studied many types of laws pertaining to judiciary, crime, punishment, contracts, inheritance, family property and adultery, etc.

After going through the encyclopaedic work of Kane, it can safely be argued that he is to great extent objective and rational while studying the *Srimitis* and *sastras*. But Kane is not entirely free from the general tenets of nationalist historiography including some of its shortcomings. Derrett superbly sums up the contributions and assessment of Kane when he says, 'The only man who set himself to explain, what the *dharma-sastra* taught and at the same time, to sketch the developments during the British period was P.V. Kane whose gigantic and solid encyclopaedia still daunts even the best-intentioned enquirer. Kane's objectivity and accuracy were phenomenal; but he too had a motive, namely to show that India's own jurisprudence should be seen in its historical setting, and when judged by the appropriate criteria, it could stand comparison with any system likely to be compared with it.[37]

After the independence, the historiography of concept of ancient Indian law continued with similar amount of publications. The prominent names to contribute in the field are N.C. Sen Gupta (*Evolution of Ancient Indian Law*, 1953), Radhabinod Pal (*The History of Hindu Law*, 1958), U.C. Sircar (*Epochs in Hindu Law*, 1958), Shivaji Singh (*Evolution of Smriti Law*, 1972), Dr Achchey Lal (*Pracheen Hindu Vidhi*, 1981), Chakradhar Jha

(*History and Sources of Law in Ancient India*, 1987) B.N. Mani (*The Laws of Dharmasastras*, 1989) and many others. Since, in the post-independent period, nationalist charm was not of that degree as it was in the colonial period, there emerged a comparatively more balanced approach to analyse various aspects of law in ancient India.

B.N. Mani studies the concept of law in the light of already existing interpretations. He accepts the fact that in *Dharmasastras*, religious, moral and legal rules are mixed together and it is not easy to draw clear line between them.[38] However, he explains it in the context of law-givers own perception. He says, 'it was a necessary corollary of *Dharmasastrakar*'s definition of law or *Dharma*, i.e., the totality of rules governing the social order. In fact, any attempt to take out completely any secular matter from its religious moorings would fail to present a complete picture of the order.[39] In his opinion, too, main sources of law are *Sruti, Smriti*, customs and self-satisfaction. *Sruti* represents immutable Divine law while *Smritis*, with their dynamic interpretations and custom were capable of incorporating changes. He remarks, 'By ascribing the origin of law to God and recognizing sources capable of introducing innovations in it without any avowed transgression (of theory), Hindu law-givers worked out a lasting reconciliation between stability and change.'[40]

However, in the post-independence era, a more dominant school of ancient Indian studies has been that of Marxists, though its beginning can well be traced in the period of the nationalist movement. Distinct from their imperialist and nationalist counterparts, Marxist historians applied the new tools and paradigm of interpretation of ancient India in general and its law in particular. Mode of production, socio-economic structure, class-struggle and dialectic materialism began to be searched in ancient India by historians like S.A. Dange and D.D. Kosambi. Ram Sharan Sharma and Romila Thapar, among many others represented this view in later generation of Marxist historiography. Romila Thapar in her book *From Lineage to State* gives an in-depth study of state-formation and its prerequisites. She explains the concept of law in ancient India in relation to customs and remarks, 'The observance of customary rules is gradually formalized, often resulting in the codification of laws.'[41]

Ram Sharan Sharma in his well-researched book *Aspects of Political Ideas and Institutions in Ancient India* has opined on the concept of law at different places. He examines the value of different literary sources for the study of ancient Indian law. In his view, Manu and Yajnavalakya contain sections on expiations and ethical code which will not be regarded as law from the modern point of view, but the works of Narada. Brhaspati and Katyayana are almost exclusively legal texts.[42] As said above, Jolly too has emphasized on exclusive nature of a legal text present in *Narad Smriti*. Many scholars claim that *dharma-sutra* attributed to Gautam is the most ancient.[43] While R.S. Sharma observes that of the four law books, those of Apastamba's and Baudhayana's seem to have been the oldest and not of Gautam's as is generally supposed.[44] The justification for this conclusion is many of Gautam's progressive social provisions such as Brahamanas can also lend the money – which are not found in earlier *Dharma-sutras*.

Prof. Sharma focuses on *Varna* and caste factor in the concept of ancient Indian Law. He rejects the view of many scholars who attributed the skill of Brahamanas as the reason for their appointment as judges. He tries to establish that

> 'Judges were to be recruited on caste basis ... prominent feature of Brahmanical law code is its class legislation.[45]

Accepting the actual prevalence of biased legislation, he observes that

> 'class-legislation was not a paper business but actually worked in practice unless sufficient evidence to the contrary is forthcoming it is difficult to believe that it was merely normative'.[46]

Prof. Sharma sees a gradual improvement in laws in the different phases of ancient Indian polity. He says that *Kautilya* tries to lessen the rigours of class legislation found in *Dharmasutras* while announcing capital punishment for the Brahamans also in certain case. In his words, 'Between the beginning of discriminatory laws with the early law-books and their climax with *Manu, Kautilya*'s legislation introduces a liberal interlude, its object being to provide a scheme of imperial laws overriding petty consideration of caste.[47] He also remarks that the law books of Gupta period again softened some of discriminatory regulations; leading to some improvement in the legal status of the fourth *Varna*.[48] Treading the general path of Marxist historiography, Prof. Sharma has explained these changes in light of socio-economic processes having a political outcome.

It is important to note that most Marxist historians have never followed Marxian model as it is, instead they have used it as a method of historical analysis. They have rejected the Marx's periodization of history into six eras and his notion of 'Unchanging East' in Indian context. This led Marxist historians to view the changing nature of concept of law in ancient India. So on the end result, they seem closer to nationalist historians asserting on legal reforms or dynamism in Hindu law. Both the conclusions, though dependent on mutually divergent mode of interpretation, refute the imperialist assumption of 'stagnant law' of Hindus. But Marxists' emphasis on caste and class elements among others in ancient Indian law, differentiate them fundamentally with their nationalist counterparts and bring in vicinity with imperialists (namely Maine) who highlight the undue dominance of priestly class in legal matters.

Thus, it can safely be argued that in addition to denouncing the ideas of imperialism and nationalism, Marxist historians adopted their own distinct materialistic approaches while studying the concept of law in ancient India. It is also noteworthy that Marxist historiography of the ancient Indian law has not been as enriched as it has been on socio-economic subjects. The reason behind it is perhaps the theory of 'base structure' and 'super-structure' which treats politico-legal institutions among many others, as dependent on and/or reflective of mode of production in the light of 'economic determinism'.

The post-independence era also witnessed the change of perception in western world in its outlook towards Indian past. After the collapse of imperialism across the globe, the political as well as cultural superiority of Europe was no more unchallenged. Post-war period facilitated new intellectual movements namely, post-modernism, deconstructionism, etc., (which are described in first chapter) which made Westerners to revisit their account of Indian past. Therefore, the post-independent Europeans writings are not swept by imperialist stereotypes and reflect a more sensitive and comparatively impartial approaches and tendencies in general while studying the concept of law of ancient India.

The important European Indologists of this new paradigm and period are French Robert Lingat and British J.D.M. Derrett. Lingat's book entitled *The Classical Law of India* is regarded by many (like Derrett) as the best book ever written on the subject. The book begins with the analysis of the nature of *Dharma* and its significance in determining the origin, nature and functioning of law in ancient India.

Lingat thinks that the law in the legal system of India does not owe its origin to written sources. He writes, 'Its development was nothing either to positive law in the sense of a legislative act, or to a judicial decisions. Significantly, the rich vocabulary of Sanskrit does not contain a term corresponding to our world law or *droit* (in French).'[49] He observes that Hindus derived it (law) from a more general notion which exceeds the domain of law in many respects, i.e., duty (*Dharma*). They taught people the rules of conduct which they ought to observe by reason of their position in society and among these rules the rules of law are to be found.[50] The relation between law and the rules of conduct is clearly pronounced when Lingat observes, 'this (*dharma*) is the totality of duties which bears upon the individual according to his status (*varna*) and stage of life (*asrama*) at which he stands'.[51]

Lingat believes that in the post-Vedic period, the many rituals and sacrifices were questioned and attempts were also made to regulate the social life of men by pronouncing certain code of conduct. The result of such attempt was the compilation of earliest *Dharma-sutras*.[52] He strongly believes that the study of *Dharma-sutras* is essential if we are to do justice to the atmosphere which surrounded the birth of law in India and which impregnated it forever afterwards.[53] To quote Lingat again 'If great part of what we call personal legal status is found amongst the precepts of *achara*, the criminal law appears in turn in large measure in the theory of sins and penances'.[54]

Lingat compares the form and content of *Dharmasutras* with those of *Dharmasastras*. Unlike the sutras which are compiled in prose-style, *Dharmasastras* are written in verse-form. As for content, *Dharmasastras* deal with the same subject as the *Dharmsutras*, but they are much more extensive work and give much larger place to rules of juridical character.[55] However the real significant point in the development of juridical science, believes Lingat was the compilation of *commentaries* and *digests* (*nibandhas*) which follow the *Dharmasastras*. He observes,

> 'The appearance of the commentaries and digests marks an important phase – perhaps we ought to say a turning point – in the evaluation of juridical thought in India. A technique of interpretation is there put to work and is applied without alteration until the British period began and even thereafter it is no exaggeration to say that it was only with that interpretation that a true juridical science began in India'.[56]

Lingat believes that apart from written rules of *Dharmasastra*, customs, too, played an important role in the development of juridical law. In this regard, he says that the rule of *Dharma* did not become a juridical rule until it entered into social behaviour and was accepted by the population as a customary rule. Like many nationalist scholars, he too believes that the theory of *kali-varjya* reflected the influence of custom on *dharma* and served to follow changes that took place in opinion and manners.[57] But at the same time Lingat rejects the idea of many scholars such as Nelson that Hindu law was entirely customary and *Dharmasastras* were purely literary works. He remarks:

> 'Written laws of the *sastras* and customary laws of different groups of humanity thus existed side by side and were equally respected though often in notable disagreement with each other. The former acted upon the latter and restricted its mobility; but the latter also acted upon the former through the medium of interpretation.'[58]

J.D.M. Derrett is also an important European Indologist who penned books and articles about ancient Indian laws. He was not only free from imperialist prejudices but also criticized scholars like James Mill. He termed the book of Mill as 'disastrous' and laments that most of the Indologists of the 19th century 'imbibed the views and notions of James Mill.[59] Derrett approaches the study of legal history quite dispassionately and analyses any legal concept in its totality. He refutes the view that ancient Indians were unaware of the science of jurisprudence and remarks that the study of jurisprudence commenced in India about three millennia ago, out of the problems created by political merging of communities of common cultural heritage but diverging practices on the one hand, and of Aryan or sub-Aryan with Dravidians, Kolarian and other indigenous peoples, on the other.[60]

In Derrett's observation, imperialist historians are far from true while regarding ancient Indian law as stagnant, unpractical, incomplete, eternal and immutable. Similarly, he did not believe that the Brahmans, who were the compilers of law, were tyrannous and exploited the docile population. He believes that in addition to their education, it was the inherited skill of Brahmans to manage the complicated sacrifices and fulfil the function with purity that enabled them to be appointed as the jurists.[61] It is to be noted that in R.S. Sharma's view Brahamanas were recruited as judges on the basis of caste only.

Derrett also does not subscribe to the hypothesis that religion had an overbearing influence on the legal system of ancient India. He argues that religion merely assisted the formulation and rationalization of law ... it affected legal rules chiefly by way of facilitating reforms.[62] He is of the opinion that if religious and legal matters were treated by the same, it was because in India 'right' and the legally enforceable were regarded as intimately connected topics. Citing instances from the laws of marriage, adoption, debt and succession, Derrett remarks that in every case, the rule aims at an object which was objectively worthy of attainment; and religious arguments which support it is of formal utility but of no substantial value.[63] In his view, the relationship between religious doctrine and the rules of substantive law is not that of cause and effect, but rather that of form and substance.[64] Like many Indologists, he too studied the relation between the law and custom. He says that custom in order to be able to influence the law must be old, related to a social group or locality, followed as a matter of obligation and not repudiated abandoned by the party relying upon it.[65] Regarding the relation between the *sastra* and custom, Derret comments, the *sastra* incorporated numerous customs inevitably, since it was itself the fruit of customs systematized, compared and summarily set down.[66]

This changed approach can well be seen in many contemporary American historians of India namely, Charles Drekmeier. He in his book *Kingship and Community in Early India* (1962) has devoted a chapter entitled 'The Codes of Dharmasastra' to the study of ancient Indian law. He does not agree to assumption of Maine that *Dharmasastras* signify an ideal situation and had nothing to do with actual practices. In his words, 'How closely the *smritis* reflect the actual laws and rules of society cannot be determined from archaeological records, but as commentaries on the *Vedas*; and as a valid aspect of tradition in their own right, they were accepted as authoritative in the administration of justice and the prescription of duty. It is not entirely accurate to say, as Sir Henry Maine does, that the codes represent an ideal picture rather than a reflection of the political scene of the time.[67] Similarly, on the basis of his study of different sources of ancient Indian law, mainly *Vedas, Smririts*, customs, Drekmeier refutes the stereotype pertaining to 'stagnant law'. He says, 'The Dharmasastra literature and the general theory of Hindu law also reveal an occasional readiness to make law respond to the changing needs of the community.'[68]

Drekmeier refers to the fact that basically ancient Indian law was conceived as God-given, as codified and interpreted by learned men, versed in the Vedic tradition. In the event of dispute over the interpretation of *Vedas*, a council (*parishad*) of up to ten Brahamana sages was to be convened. This led Drekmeier to remark, 'Thus, in the last analysis Hindu law was what men agreed that it was. But consensus honours certain first principles which remain fairly constant, the consequences of man's aspiration, his need for consistency and for an explanation of the universe in which he lives.'[69] This interpretation of the nature of ancient Indian law by many historians, including Drekmeier, reminds us of the well-known case of 'Keshavanand Bharthi versus State of Kerala' (1973) in independent India. In this case the Hon'ble Supreme Court of India passed a historic judgment that parliament is empowered to amend the constitution in accordance with Article 368 of the Constitution, but in no way it can tamper with the basic structure of the constitution.[70]

This kind of stability, coupled with timely and necessary accommodation without compromising fundamental theory, is to be founded in early Indian law. Perhaps this is the point which many post-independence historians try to highlight while rejecting the stereotype of 'stagnant Hindu law', in their ancient Indian legal studies.

The post-independence historiography of law in ancient India is further enriched by the Russian Indologist W.F. Menski who is considered an authority *on Indian law* and comparative legal history. His book *Hindu Law: Beyond Tradition and Modernity* (2003) is an intensively researched book that examines the development of Hindu law from ancient period through its drastic remoulding in the colonial era, to its emergence as a post-modern entity in 21st century. He argues that it would be wrong to see Hindu law as uniformly oppressive.[71] He, too, contends against stagnancy of Hindu law and delineates it as a living and ever-dynamic phenomenon. In his words, 'Hindu Law is very much alive and playing a role even in the current post-modern environment as is apparent in the way the courts themselves interpret various aspects of law including the rules of inheritance, marriage, maintenance and divorce.'[72]

Very recently another Indologist Donald R. Davis, Jr. authored *The Spirit of Hindu Law* (2010). N.R. Madhav Menon reviewed it in the *The Hindu*, and it is there we come to know the basic assumptions of Davis. The author has adopted an inter-disciplinary approach and comparative methodology in his study of the concept of ancient Indian law. For Davis, 'law is the theology of ordinary life' and the European notion of law, as rules backed by sanctions enforced by the state, is an unnatural idea produced at a certain moment of history to serve colonial objectives.[73] Among the merits of the concept of Hindu law, he identifies the fact that it acknowledges and explains the gap between 'rule' and 'behaviour' in everyday life and highlights the higher purpose involved whenever law is invoked.[74]

Davis observes that the true nature of law lies in its integral relationship with religion, though the two are different entities and have different roles to play in society. Despite several centuries of deliberate secularization, the state could not remove elements of religion from the law even in nations that are most secular, liberal and democratic.[75] He asserts, 'The legal concepts central to Euro-American scholarship do not exhaust the rich legacy of ancient legal systems. Delving deep into the history of Hindu religious traditions has not been a fashionable venture with scholars. The need to know the details of Hindu law for the sake of a 'colonial administration has put us in the habit of only learning *about* Hindu law, and not *from* it'.[76]

This kind of reflections leaves no doubt on the fact that the post-colonial and contemporary Indologists are highly careful and respectful in their conception of ancient Indian law. At the methodological level, they substantiate their interpretations, drawing support from authoritative Sanskrit texts, relate them to the total Hindu tradition and finally bring out its importance and relevance. Indeed, it is a type of total revisiting of Western vision of Indian past.

It now becomes obvious that as colonialist requirements and racial superiority pervaded the imperialist assumption of ancient Indian law earlier, idealization of ancient Indian concept of law to strengthen the national movement was the guiding principle for the nationalist historians. Marxist scholars tried to judge the law of Ancient India on the basis of a materialistic view of history. But it is to be noted that in a country like India where religio-legal tradition is deeply rooted, concept of law cannot be explained well, terming it a mere 'superstructure'. Since the emergence of a decolonized world, there has been a shift in approaches of historians across the globe which resulted in a more objective, refreshing and critical studies of the notion of law in Ancient India. This new trend represented mainly by Lingat, Derrett and Davis along with some contemporary Indian scholars can provide us a better understanding of the concept of ancient Indian law in its pertinent historical perspective. So for as the ultimate or final study is concerned, it is neither possible nor desirable in the discipline of historiography.

Notes

1. Mill, James, *The History of British India*, Vol. I, p. 155
2. Ibid., p. 157
3. Ibid., p. 161
4. Ibid., p. 196
5. Thapar, Romila, *Past and Prejudice*, p. 10.
6. Maine, Sir Henry Sumner, Quoted in J.D.M. Derrett's *Religion Law and State in India*, p. 22–23
7. Maine, Sir Henry Sumner, *Ancient Law*, p. 7.
8. Ibid., p. 7.
9. Ibid., p. 171.
10. Ibid., p. 17–18.
11. Gopal, Lallanji, in Introduction to Achchey Lal's *Pracheen Hindu Vidhi*, p. xvi.
12. Jolly, J., *Minor Law Books*, part I, p. xiii.
13. Ibid., p. pxv.
14. ——. *Hindu Law and Customs*, p. 1.
15. Buhler, G., The Laws of Manu, S.B.E., Vol. XXV, p. XLVI.
16. Ibid., p. XLVI.
17. Jayaswal, K.P., *Hindu Polity*, p. 310.
18. Aiyangar, K.V.R., Quoted in J.D.M. Derrett's op. cit., p. 76.
19. Banerjee, P.N., *Public Administration in Ancient India*, p. 216.
20. Dikshitar, V.R.R., *Hindu Administrative Institutions*, p. 219.
21. Jayaswal, K.P. op. cit., p. 317.

22. Kane, P.V., Quoted in Robert Lingat's *The Classical Law of India*, p. 14.
23. Ghoshal, U.N., *A History of Indian Political Ideas*, p. 9.
24. Ibid., p. 11.
25. Ibid., p. 11.
26. Ibid., p. 13.
27. Sen, P.N., *General Principles of Hindu Jurisprudence*, 375–376.
28. P.V. Kane, *History of Dharmasastra* Vol. III, p. 24.
29. Ibid., p. 244.
30. Ibid., pp. 244–245
31. Ibid., p. 258
32. Mill, James, op. cit., p. 157.
33. Kane, P.V., op. cit., p. 259.
34. *India 2010*, Publication Dept., Ministry of Information and Broadcasting, Govt. of India, p. 763.
35. P.V. Kane, op. cit., p. 267–268.
36. Ibid., pp. 866–867.
37. Derrett, J.D.M. in Translator's Preface in *The Classical Law India*, p. ix.
38. Mani, B.N., in preface to *Laws of Dharmasastras.*
39. Ibid.
40. Ibid., p. 6.
41. Thapar, Romila, *From Lineage to State*, p. 12.
42. Sharma, R.S., *Aspects of Political Ideas and Institutions in Ancient India*, p. 18.
43. Lingat, Robert, op. cit., p. 19.
44. Sharma, R.S., op. cit., p. 16.
45. Ibid., pp. 243–244.
46. Ibid., p. 247.
47. Ibid., p. 246.
48. Ibid., pp. 245–246.

49. Lingat, Robert, op. cit., p. xii.
50. Ibid., p. xii.
51. Ibid., p. 4.
52. Ibid., p. 18.
53. Ibid., p. 28.
54. Ibid., p. 63.
55. Ibid., p. 73.
56. Ibid., p. 143.
57. Ibid., p. 194.
58. Ibid., p. 141–142.
59. Derrett, J.D.M., *Essays in Classical and Modern Hindu Law*, Vol. 2, p. 42–43.
60. Ibid., 47–48.
61. Ibid., p. 49.
62. Ibid., p. 50.
63. ——. *Religon Law and the State in India*, p. 104.
64. Ibid., p. 117.
65. Ibid., p. 157.
66. Ibid., p. 158.
67. Drekmeier, Charles., *Kingship and Community in Early India*, p. 228.
68. Ibid., p. 234.
69. Ibid., p. 235.
70. Kashyap, Subhash., *Our Constiutution*, p. 266.
71. Menski, W.F., *Hindu Law: Beyond Tradition and Modernity*, p. 3.
72. Ibid., p. 4.
73. Davis, Donald, R. Jr., *The Sprit of Hindu Laws*, Book Review published in *The Hindu* (New Delhi edition), 31 May 2011.
74. Ibid.
75. Ibid.
76. Ibid.

3

Interpretations of Social Legislation in Ancient India

The society is considered the expansion of family at a larger level. Social life is governed more by conventions than the canons of law. But in ancient India, law-makers had a great concern for smooth family life, moral values and day-to-day practices in accordance with *Dharma*. Therefore, they made elaborate provisions to regulate society and family, which have been commented upon keenly by the modern historians.

Creation of Social Order

The most striking feature of any society lies in its structure of hierarchy. It is this hierarchy or social order that to a great extent shapes the nature and course of other characteristics of social life. In India, social hierarchy is institutionalised by the system of *varna* and caste. The earliest mention of all the four *varnas* is found in the tenth book of *Rigveda* wherein the *Brahamana, Kshatriya, Vaishya* and *Shudra* are said to have originated from the mouth, arm, thigh and leg of *Purusha*, respectively. Initially, the *Varna* system came to being for the convenience of functional division in the Rig Vedic period. But later, owing to the complex historical processes, it converted into a birth-based institution, paving the way for the growth of a rigid caste-system.

The ancient legal texts played a crucial role in theorizing such a process of social transformation. Historically, *varna* or caste identity has decided not only one's social and political status but also the economic or occupational sphere. This multi-dimensional implication of Indian social order has attracted innumerable scholars from India and abroad to study it. Here, it is neither feasible nor required to discuss the entire history-writing of caste-system, since it is a subject more of a social history, but studies adopting a legalist approach or Dharmasastric view can well be mentioned.

The credit to initiate the tradition of modern studies on the social order goes to the officials of East India Company. It was necessary for their administrative purposes to have an acquaintance with social system of foreign nationals whom they have to rule. *A Code of Gentoo Laws* (1776) is among the earlier books which can be associated to some extent with the social history of ancient India. But it was the utilitarian philosopher James Mill who laid down the first systematic account of early Indian social order. Mill, owing to his utilitarian belief and coupled with imperialist vision, is highly critical of every aspect of Indian history such as polity, laws, religion, manners, etc., so is the attitude with society as well.

Mill, commenting on the four varnas, says that the classification instituted by the author of the Hindu laws is the first and simplest form of the division of labour and employments[1]. He adds, 'On this division of the people, and the privileges or disadvantages annexed to the several castes, the whole frame of Hindu society so much depends, that it is an object of primary importance, and merits a full elucidation'[2]. He holds the view that the stratification into castes is characterised by the stark differences in rights and privileges between the Brahmens (sic) and Sudras. He writes, 'The priesthood is generally found to usurp the greatest authority, in the lowest state of society .... The Brahmens among the Hindus have acquired and maintained an authority, more exalted, more commanding, and extensive, than the priests have been able to engross among any other portion of mankind.'[3] Mill attributes Brahmanas' superiority to the frequent performance of an 'infinite and burdensome ritual' whose sole judges and directors were Brahmanas.[4]

Contrasting the status of Sudras with that of Brahmanas, Mill remarks, 'As much as the Brahmen (sic) is an object of intense veneration, so much is the Sudra an object of contempt, and even of abhorrence, to the other classes of his countrymen.'[5] He further says, 'The business of the Sudras is servile labour, and their degradation inhuman. Not only is the most abject and grovelling submission imposed upon them as a religious duty, but they are driven from their just and equal share in all the advantages of the social institution.'[6]

Mill's ideas are highly disputable at some grounds. Not to speak of nationalist historians of later period, his publisher and noted Indologist H.H. Wilson himself has corrected or modified many of Mill's views. For example, Wilson questions the use of the term 'abhorrence' (for *Sudras)*, since the law does not justify it, and says, 'Mr. Mill has collected the extreme texts, and has passed over all the favourable or qualifying passages.'[7] He added, 'The condition of a Sudra, in the Hindu system, was infinitely preferable to that of the helot, the slave, or the serf of the Greek, the Roman, and the feudal systems. He (Sudra) was independent, his services were optional: they were not agricultural, but domestic and personal, and claimed adequate compensation.'[8]

This juxtaposition displays not only the critique of Mill's inaccuracies but also the different perception of Indian society by Indologist which is best manifested in Max Müller's romanticism about Indian culture. Despite many limitations, it was Mill's views and conclusions which came to be popularised and followed by company officers and most European writers. The reason behind can well be searched in light of the need of British Imperialism which was ideologically based on the hypothesis of 'Indian backwardness', justifying so-called 'The White Man's Burden'.

Sir Henry Maine, the great legal historian, was inspired by Mill to study Indian past; and he accordingly reflects some of latter's opinions. He condemned caste system thus: 'Division into classes which at a particular crisis of social history is necessary for the maintenance of the national existence degenerates into the most disastrous and blighting of all human institutions: Caste'.[9] But his approaches to Indian society reflect the basic tenets of his school of historical jurisprudence as well. He in his another book *Village Communities in the East and West* viewed the early Indian social order with a prism of legal evolutionism. Therein, he opined, 'Caste is merely a name for trade or occupation, and the sole tangible effect of the Brahminical theory is that it creates a religious sanction for what is really a primitive and natural distribution of classes .... The true view of India is that, as a whole, it is divided into a vast number of independent, self-acting, organised social groups – trading, manufacturing, cultivating.'[10]

Romanticist historian Mountstuart Elphinstone by and large echoed Mill's propositions. For him, the most striking feature of ancient Indian society is its caste system. He says that the first feature that strikes us in the society described by Manu is the division into four classes or castes (the sacerdotal, the military, the industrious and the servile).[11] Underlying the privileged position of Brahmans, he writes, 'the interpretation of law is expressly confined to Brahmins'.[12] The property of the sacred class is as well-protected by law as its powers.[13]

The social order of early India was studied not only by historians but also by a great number of sociologists, anthropologists, social philosophers and many others. Senart has brought for the first time to the attention of the European world the fact that a caste and a *varna* are not identical. He described caste as a close corporation, in theory at any rate, rigorously hereditary; equipped with a certain traditional and independent organization including a chief and a council.[14] But the existence of 'close corporation' and 'councils' is disputable. Sir H. Risely attributed the origin of caste system to the racial differences between Indo-European Aryans and indigenous people[15] and G.H. Ghurye termed it as 'Brahmanic child of the Indo-Aryans of Ganga Velly'.[16] Louis Dumont has forcefully argued in his *Homo Hierarchicus* that Hindu (Brahmanic) ideology of 'purity' and 'pollution' provides the real determining and organizing factor behind caste system.[17]

Thus, it is evident that most western scholars often perceived the social order of early India as the outcome of Brahmans' religious framework, and its dominant feature being the dire differences among various strata of this hierarchy. But such attitude seems to have undergone change in the post-war intellectual atmosphere of the later half of 20th century, as reflected in the writings of some contemporary legal historians. French scholar Robert Lingat adopts a balanced view while studying the creation and transformation of Varna into caste (*jati*). He, regarding the functions assigned to four *Varnas*, says: 'The hierarchy between the functions does not prevent their being strictly complementary to each other. Each *varna* is equally necessary to social order. Each relies or even leans on three others. Thus a vaisya or a sudra is fully quit of his social duty if he accomplishes his allotted task, however humble it may be. Our texts promise him then, as recompense, the prospect of being reborn in a higher caste. At the same time they threaten the member of higher castes who neglect their duties with rebirth in an inferior caste.'[18]

The transformation of *varna* into birth-based caste has been viewed by many like Senart as a deliberate deed by Brahmans to secure their supremacy under the *varna* system. Senart wrote that the castes were superimposed on a regime, to which they were originally strangers, less by any organic development than by an intellectual construction.[19] But for Lingat, 'It is not free from a tendency which Senart himself rightly condemned in other Indologists, namely to see everywhere the priest's hand, and to attribute a much exaggerated importance to the priest's influence upon the organisation of society.'[20]

Lingat, taking the cue from Dumezil's research, asserts that:

> 'the first three *varnas* correspond to a very ancient tradition to a tripartite conception of the world and of a society which turns up at the very foundations of the majority of European nations .... 'This is the conception which India had expressed in her turn by representing the whole Aryan community as divided into brahmans, kshatriyas and vaisyas. Our brahmans did not have to invent it'.[21]

He also observes that:

'there are only four varnas, although the number of castes is unlimited (Manu, x, 4). In modern India, where castes proliferate, it is impossible to reduce them to so simple a framework as the Brahminical theory. The *varna* of the Brahmins holds its ground, no doubt; yet it does not constitute a caste, but rather castes distinct from each other'.[22]

The western judgements on early Indian social organization came as a challenge to Indian scholars. Though, parallel to the criticism of caste-system, there has been a group of European scholars like Sidney Low, Meredith Townsend and G.H. Mease, and so on, who conceived an appreciative opinion of this Indian institution. These were the thinkers who got disillusioned with the extreme materialistic lifestyle of post-industrial revolution period, and were in search of some old Indian ideals to rebalance their contemporary society. But the biggest challenge to Western condemnation of ancient Indian social order came from Indian historians, often termed as 'nationalists'. They, generally inspired by contemporaneous Indian Nationalist Movement, emerged with their own viewpoint of social ideas and institutions of ancient India.

R.C. Dutt tried to explain the evolution of caste system by taking into account the 'soft climate' of Gangetic valley which caused Aryans lose their vigour of a conquering race.[23] He wrote,

> 'The priestly class increased in number and in influence, until they formed a hereditary caste of their own. The kings and warriors of the Gangetic valley ... soon separated themselves from the people and formed a caste of their own. The mass of the people – the vaisyas or visas of the *Rig Veda* – became more feeble than their forefathers in the Punjab, and wore, without a protest, the chains which priests and warriors through around them. And as subjection means demoralisation, the people in Hindu kingdoms never afterwards became what the people in ancient and modern Europe have striven to be. And lastly, the aborigines who were subjugated and had adopted the Aryan civilisation formed the low caste of sudras.'[24]

Dutt asserts that Hindu writers never completely lost sight of the fact that caste was originally only a distinction based on professions,[25] and against the much alleged divisive feature of caste-system, he states, 'Caste reserved some privileges for priests, and some privileges for warriors, in ancient times; but never divided and disunited the Aryan people'.[26] There are numerous passages in the *Brahmana* literature which show that the distinctions between the castes were by no means so rigid in the early times as at a later period.[27] But great amount of prohibited degrees in the marriage rules among others contradicts this projected flexibility of caste system.

U.N. Ghoshal observes that theories of Brahmanical privileges and immunities as found in *Smritis* are due to the application of Vedic belief in the highest origin of this caste.[28] P.V. Kane in the volume II, part I., of his encyclopaedic *History of Dharmasastra* presented a detailed study of various aspects of ancient Indian social order. He does not think that the caste system was an artificial product due to the intrigues, greed and cunning of Brahamanas.[29]

Kane contradicts Ghurye's view that *Brahamans* had become a caste in Vedic period itself. In his findings, 'These verses (Vedic hymns) may be conceded as pointing to the existence of three groups (*Brahamanas, kshatriyas* and *Vishah*) but there is nothing in them to show that these three had crystallised into somewhat like the castes of later times.'[30] He observes that even in the *Purushashukta* (Rigveda, x, 90) where the words *brahamana*, *rajanya* and *vaishya* occur, the word *varna* is not used. Hence, one may reasonably say that the only watertight groups that are positively or expressly vouchsafed by the *Rig Veda* are *Arya* and *Dasa* or *Dasyu*.[31]

Kane has argued strongly in favour of the creation of a social order in the form of *Varna* system. He claims, 'the theory of *varnas* as conceived by *Manu* and other *smritikaras* was based upon the idea of the division of the labour, on the idea of balancing the rival claims of various sections of society; it laid greatest emphasis upon the duties of the *varnas* rather than upon their rights and privileges'.[32]

Kane questions the notion that criticises *Smriti* view of the derivation of numerous castes from the mixture (*samkara*) of the four *varnas* as 'purely hypothetical and imaginary'. He notes,

> 'the numerous castes mentioned in the *Smritis* did exist at the time of *Smritis* ... that the peculiar avocations and means of livelihood assigned to various castes reflected the real state of things. The element of hypothesis and speculation lies only in the theory of a particular sub-caste having sprung from the union of two persons belonging to two particular *varnas* or castes'.[33]

Here the role of legal texts is reduced to mere conceptualizing the existing practices, and this idea, as mentioned above, is upheld by Lingat also.

Kane, commenting on the peculiar doctrines of *Jatytkarsha* (rise in status as a caste) and *jatyapakarsh*, (fall in status as a caste) says that these provisions would considerably lessen the rigour of the caste system based purely on birth but admits that due to difficulty in remembering the descent for five or seven generations (as was required in the doctrines) it remained as an ideal.[34]

The privileges of *Brahmanas*, juxtaposed with the innumerable disabilities of *Sudras*, have been vehemently censured by many Western writers like James Mill. In this regard, Kane not only defends the special rights assigned to *Brahamanas* but also arouses sympathy for them. He points out, 'the ideal before *Brahmanas* was to lead a life of comparative poverty; they were forbidden to follow many worldly pursuits and depended on the generosity of their patrons .... In modern capitalist societies those who have brains and knowledge tend to become financiers and capitalists'.[35]

Pertaining to the legal status of *Sudra*, he comments, 'If the *Sudra* laboured under certain grave disabilities, he had certain compensating advantages. He could follow almost any profession except the few especially reserved for *brahmanas* and *kshatriyas*. The *sudra* was free from the round of countless daily rites. He was compelled to undergo no *samskara* (except marriage), he had to undergo no penances for lapses from the rules of the *sastras*, he had to observe no restrictions of *gotra* and *pravara* in marriage'.[36] It seems as if Kane interprets disabilities as a kind of freedom of *sudras*, and then enthusiastically states,

'Those western writers who turn up their nose at the position of *sudra* in ancient and medieval India conveniently forget what atrocious crimes were perpetrated by their people in the institution of slavery and in their dealings with the red Indians and other backward colour races;[37] slavery was prevalent partially in early India also but as Kane himself shows it was 'more flexible and humane institution than its European counterpart.'[38]

Kane has discussed the issues of 'untouchability' in the light of ancient Indian legal texts. To him, untouchability did not and does not arise by birth alone. It arises in various ways, such as: sinful acts, religious hatred, filthy avocations, taboo contacts, etc.[39] He concludes, 'these restrictions were not inspired by hardness of heart or any racial or caste pride, as is often said, but they were due to psychological or religious views and the requirements of hygiene'[40]. He further says, 'As many professions and crafts were in ancient times hereditary, gradually the idea arose that a man who belonged to a caste pursuing certain filthy or abhorred avocations or crafts was by birth untouchable.'[41]

Thus, among the Indian authority on legal texts it is P.V. Kane to whom in-depth study of social order can be attributed. But his approach too, to great extent, seems influenced by general tendency of nationalist historians. He tries to justify the many biased social trend of Indian society either by quoting some balancing provisions or by reminding of more severe European practices. But it is to be remembered that blunders done by others can't be excuses for mistakes of ours. Further, even if we believe that caste existed in social reality and was not a deliberate creation of *Brahmana*, the question remains unanswered that why the element of caste consideration by *smritikaras* pervaded every walk of life, be it marriage, sonship, education, rituals, punishment and interest-rates. Here, concerning rules are skewedly in favour of upper castes. Nevertheless, the erudite survey of Sanskrit texts on the subject is undisputedly great contribution by Kane to the generations of scholars.

Historiography of the social hierarchy of ancient India is further enriched with new approaches and theories by historians owing allegiance to Marxist ideology. There are a number of Marxist historians including S.A. Dange and D.D. Koshambi who studied different aspects of early Indian society with materialistic line of historical research, but it is mainly Romila Thapar and R.S. Sharma who utilised relevant Dharmsastic literature to great extent to explore ancient Indian society. R.S. Sharma sketches the various stages of the evolution of social order in the light of material progress, instead of treating it as a particular historical event.

First, R.S. Sharma evaluates the different theories regarding the origin of the caste system. In his opinion, the theory that attributes division of human beings into four categories to the natural aptitudes and endowments overlooks the social and material environment wherein these are nurtured.[42] Second theory emphasising on the notions of purity and impurity for the evolution of caste does not realise the fact that primitive and ancient societies outside India did not give rise to caste system, despite having similar notions.[43] Another theory which accounts for the origin of the caste system in terms of the division of labour ignores the hereditary aspects of this system.[44]

After this assessment, Sharma states his own proposition regarding the emergence of the institution of caste. He says,

> 'The origin and growth of the caste system can be better appreciated if we bear in mind that caste is a form of social differentiation. Since social differentiation arises out of social conflicts and unequal distribution of resources and produce, the origin and growth of the caste cannot be understood without a study of social processes which again are intimately connected with changes in material life.'[45]

With this hypothetical criterion, he sees the rise of caste from the Buddhist period marked by the expansion of agricultural economy. He notes, 'With the beginning of the wide use of iron tools for crafts and cultivation, conditions were created for the transformation of the tribal, pastoral, almost egalitarian Vedic society into a full-fledged agricultural and class-divided social order in the sixth-century BC.'[46]

Sharma believes that for enjoying the social surplus produced by the peasants, artisans, hired labourers and 'agricultural slaves' the *varna* mechanism was devised.[47] The non-performance of the functions assigned to different *varnas* or social strata by the *Dharmasasras* denotes a deep social crisis often termed as 'The Kali Age' and is mentioned around the third century AD onwards.[48] According to Sharma, mixed castes or *Varnasamkara*, whom the Brahmanical law-givers depict as the offspring of mixture between the *Varnas*, were actually tribal people annexed to the Hindu system as a Sudra caste through land grants in Gupta and post-Gupta periods.[49] Similarly, he has explained the rising rigidity in caste system in light of early medieval limitations on socio-economic mobility.[50]

Earlier P.V. Kane had interpreted the problem of untouchability on psychological, religious and hygienic grounds, but to R.S. Sharma it is due to the attitude towards manual labour. He writes, 'Brahamans were not allowed to take to the plough and manual work. Gradually the contempt of the higher varnas for manual work reached such limits that they developed hatred for the hands that practised crafts and thus came to look upon certain manual labourers as untouchables.'[51]

Thus, R.S. Sharma followed a familiar Marxist line of historical research and analysed the *varna* and caste system in ancient India as process of social formation. Historicising of social crisis and Kali Age is commendable; but associating *Varnsamkaras* to the practice of land grants is difficult to accept, since the mixture castes are mentioned even in *Sutra* texts whereto the practice of granting lands can hardly be traced. More plausible explanation for the *varnsamkara* is inter-caste marriages as a social reality, irrespective of particular economic changes. Maybe, the land grants would have opened more ways to accelerate the emergence of *Varnshankara*. Sharma's materialistic approach to the origin and growth of caste system is by and large identical with his views about the rise of state in ancient India. Both caste and state are said to have been shaped by the economic conditions of the erstwhile Buddhist era. The materialistic approach to the study of early Indian social order is further strengthened by Romila Thapar.

Romila Thapar heralded a unique idea by tracing the origin of caste system to pre-Aryan society by pointing out the absence of caste structure in any other Aryan culture of the world.[52] But even if we accept the existence of social stratification in Harappan civilization, as Thapar claims, this notion inasmuch presupposes the European connection of Vedic Aryans, is subject to debate.

She opined, 'The origin and development of caste was not controlled by the *Brahmans*. The latter were merely shrewd enough to realize that they could use the existing system to their own benefit. In accordance with their own vision of society, they enunciated laws on caste.'[53]

Thapar searches the reason for the continuity of caste system in its inbuilt structure.

> 'The fact that caste was never confronted with the shadow of its decline can be traced to the structure itself. Each caste or sub-caste formed its own independent social unit, with its own laws of survival based on the economic possibilities to which it could aspire.'[54] 'The Hindu tradition managed to maintain a considerable degree of social harmony by a careful balancing of over-all authoritarianism with local autonomy .... Dissident groups which began with the support of a cross section of society ended up by being identified as a separate sub-caste.'[55]

From the above survey, it is clear that different historians have different opinions regarding the various aspects of early Indian social order. It is such a relevant social issue that many scholars who are technically not historians have commented on it. Among such writers Mahatma Gandhi and B.R. Ambedkar stand foremost; but they differ fundamentally on the issue. The former tried to humanise the rigour of casteism and eradicate untouchability; but the latter advocated complete annihilation of caste-system and, for that, suggested legal and religious reforms.

In the historiography, the origin, growth and modification of caste system and factors behind them in different phases of history is more important than to debate its present reality. For this purpose, vast ancient legal texts provide sufficient evidence. But owing to different schools – imperialist, nationalist, Marxist – they could not be viewed unanimously, as is apparent from above discussion. It is a matter of fact that despite resistance of centuries, caste structure could not be removed; it might indicate certain beneficial and 'adaptability' aspect of this institution. At the same time, nobody can deny the big gaps in the rights of upper and lower strata within the same institution. This biased aspect of caste system not only rules out ideal of equality but also strikes at the root of humanism. Just because of being an imperialist or Marxist assumption, everything must not be viewed as wrong.

Marital Laws

Marriage is an alliance between a man and a woman recognized by law bringing deeper socio-economic impacts over the life of both particularly. It is a very significant social practice which is as old as the dawn of civilization but its nature has always been a changing trend. Sir John Lubbock has shown that marriage, as we understand it, was unknown to primitive men, and the earlier notions about it were very different from those prevailing in advanced society. He says,

> 'Marriage and the relationship of a child to its father and mother, seem to us so natural and obvious, that we are apt to look on them as aboriginal and general to the human race. This, however, is very far from being the case. The lowest races have no institution of marriage; true love is almost unknown among them; and marriage, in its lowest phases, is by no means a matter of affection and companionship.'[56]

It is generally assumed that marriage evolved with the notion of sexual union and later developed as the socio-religious institution, subordinating the physical aspect. But scholars like Westermarck conceive marriage as an economic institution as well, which in various ways affects the proprietary rights of the parties.[57]

Though marriage as a consensual union between persons of opposite sexes is a universal phenomenon, its legal implications and consequences are not the same throughout the world. In India marriage is not a mere social alliance or contract between man and women; but is one of the sixteen sacraments *samskaras* that govern the life of a Hindu from his birth to death. It is considered an indissoluble relation of two souls to be continued even after death. In brief, the Hindu law of marriage is influenced greatly by the religious beliefs of early Indians.

Owing to its deeper socio-economic and religious dimensions, the marital laws of the Hindus have always been an area of keen interest among historians. The Europeans initiated the research in this field and soon were followed by their nationalist counterparts. The Marxist historians tried to unveil the materialistic landscape of the marital laws in ancient India. So the innumerable interpretations of the early Indian marriage laws have emerged in the past almost two hundred years.

Colebrooke analysed the marital laws in the light of ancient Indian religion. He opined that in Hindu law marriage is regarded as one of the ten *samskaras*, or sacraments, necessary for regeneration of men of the twice-born classes, and the only sacrament for women and Sudras.[58] The religious character of Hindu marital laws can be pointed out by some other facts. Firstly, it is a settled doctrine of the Hindu religion that one must have a son to save him from a place of torment called *put* (*Manu,* ix, 138); marriage, as the primary means to that end, becomes a religious necessity. Secondly, the concept of three debts (*tri-rina*) makes offspring necessary to liberate a *Braḥaman* from his debt to forefathers. Along with Colebrooke, other European historians and Indologists have explained marital laws as an area of religious influence.

Sir Henry Maine has studied and compared the condition of women in ancient Indian and Roman laws. For him 'of all the chapters of entire Law of Persons the most important is that which is concerned with the status of Females'.[59] In this regard, he proposes, the notion of 'Perpetual Tutelage' of women under which a female, though relieved from her parent's authority by his decease, continues subject through life to her nearest male relations, or to her father's nominees, as her Guardian.[60] He further adds, 'In India the system survives in absolute completeness, and its operation is so strict that a Hindoo Mother frequently becomes the ward of her own sons.'[61] In

Maine's opinion, the institution of the marriage is not as significant as the idea of *Patria Potestas* or patriarchal power in ancient periods. He remarks,

> 'In truth, in the primitive view, relationship is exactly limited by *Patria Potestas*. Where *Potestas* begins, kinship begins; and therefore adoptive relatives are among the kindred. Where the *Potestas* ends, kinship ends; so that a son emancipated by his father loses all rights of agnation. And here, we have the reason why the descendants of females are outside the limits of archaic kinship.'[62] His observation is summed thus, 'the foundation of Agnation is not the marriage of Father and Mother, but the authority of the Father.'[63]

Julius Jolly is a great German Indologist who studied different aspects of marital laws such as nature, forms and consequences of marriage in his *Hindu Law and Custom*. Firstly, Jolly discusses the practice of polyandry and promiscuity. In his opinion 'it is principally only the matrimonial connection of one woman with a number of brothers. Even the well-known law (*Manu*, 9, 182) that the son of one of the several brothers may be regarded as the common son of all may refer only to group-marriage if we connect it with polyandrous connections disregarding the interpretation of the commentators'.[64] He compares polyandry of the present day with that of Sanskrit texts and observes, 'poverty and the desire of keeping family property undivided are the causes of polyandry.'[65] He states that among the Jats of the Punjab ... the wife of the eldest brother has often to accept the younger brothers as consorts, because they have no means to meet the expenses of a marriage.[66] He further remarks that polyandry is principally seen among 'non-Aryans'. Yet it cannot be proved that polyandry of the ancient times was confined among the non-Aryan tribes. Only this much may be said that the Brahmans were always jealously antagonistic to it.[67]

Jolly points out the prevalence of prostitution as found in Sanskrit literature and notes that 'the toleration of the prostitution has not hindered the growth of a strict law of marriage. The sagas about an earlier period of immorality are utilised directly to represent the lax views about legitimate and illegitimate sons as obsolete.[68] Jolly has underlined many anomalies in family laws especially in the marital laws of the Hindus. He asserts that a kind of contrast is met with in the Indian law of marriage, in which besides the extremely rigid and lofty ideal of marriage, we find matches being made by purchase or by robbery or by defrauding the women of her portion.[69] It is a matter of fact that the festive *Svayamvara* of the epics is not found in the *Smritis* and the choice of husband is allowed to the young lady only if she is not married even after her attainment of puberty. Here, Jolly explains, 'The motive in this is that the father loses his authority over the daughter through his delay in giving her away in marriage and from this point of view it is understandable why the *Brahmans* do not count the *Svayamvara* among the eight forms of marriage.'[70]

Jolly has classified various forms of marriages into two categories: aristocratic and plebeian. He delineates the *Asura* form of marriage as the purchase of women which is allowed only to *Vaisyas* and *Sudras*.[71] He points out that the bride price (*Sulka*) of this form mentioned in the *Smritis* often signifies merely a present from the bridegroom to the bride or from the husband to the wife, thus, for example, it is mentioned as a part of the *Stridhan*.[72]

Relying on the *Sutra* and *Smriti* texts, Jolly supposes the prevalence of child marriages in early India. He says,

> 'The well-known statement of Greek authors about the attainment of puberty by Indian women at the age of seven as well as the statement about six-year-old mothers of India, are wrong in this form, as puberty is generally attained in the twelfth year; but they may refer only to the observation of marriage ceremonies of seven year old brides. *Alberuni* too was astonished at the early marriages of the Hindus.'[73]

Jolly describes various hindrances of marriage such as, defects of bride (*Kanyadosha*), and body marks (*Lakshana*) of bride-groom, privileges of seniority, etc. He criticizes stress on the equality of the two concerned parties in the marriage rules. He says,

'Instead of *Savarna* frequently also the general terms – *Sajati, Samana, Sadrisha* and similar other expressions are used to express the equality of position of the two parties concerned in a marriage, and it may probably be assumed that this principle applies to those narrow societies which actually appeared already very early and supplanted the great prehistoric *varnas*.'[74]

Jolly finds that divorce is odious to the *Smriti* writers, since it is considered to be a great sin if the married couple separate on account of mutual aversion. He notes that the connection established by a public ceremony with great pomp and shows and expenses as early as possible lays the foundation of a life-long relation and it should not be broken off so slightly.[75]

Like Colebrooke, Henry Maine and Jolly, there is a number of western historians and legal writers who studied the institution of marriage in early India. For example, J.D. Mayne (*Treatise on Hindu Law and Usages*), Sir Thomas Strange (*The Elements of Hindu Law*) and Steele (*Law and Custom of Hindu Caste*) among others can be named. Many of them were inspired either by European superiority, a sub-stream of colonialism or applied the western parameters to study the marriage system in ancient India. So with the emergence of indigenous intelligentsia, often influenced by nationalist spirit, western assumptions on Hindu marital laws were either challenged or modified.

Among the Indian historians on the subject, Sir Gooroo Das Banerjee (*The Hindu Law of Marriage and Stridhana*, 2nd ed., 1896) stands foremost. Regarding the evolution of marriage, he says, 'Marriage is first a practice, then that practice grows into a custom and finally the custom passes into law.'[76] For him the promiscuity found in primitive societies is not identical with the institution of marriage. He writes, 'The essential difference between promiscuity and marriage is the exclusiveness of the latter relation; and different forms of marriage result from the different degrees of this exclusiveness.'[77] He then studies various forms of marriages depending upon the number of parties to the relation, such as polyandry, polygamy, monogamy and upon the duration of the union. He appears close to Jolly while commenting that polyandry conduces to the preservation of the race by checking over-population and consequent starvation and misery. Fraternal polyandry has its parallel in other archaic institutions, such as that of joint property.[78]

According to Banerjee, so far as the different forms of the marriages are concerned, India may be regarded as an epitome of the world, as it is in respect to the variety of its climate, flora and fauna.[79] He notes, 'So that Indian life presents almost every possible form of the conjugal relation, from the grossest polyandry verging on promiscuity, to the purest and the most rational form of monogamy.'[80]

Banerjee holds the view that apart from those legalised by custom, the Hindu law recognises eight distinct forms of marriage: *Brahma, Daiva, Arsha, Prajapatya* or *Kaya, Asura, Gandharva, Rakshasa,* and *Paisacha*. The first four are the approved forms of marriages and are almost peculiar to Brahmans while the last four are considered base or disapproved forms. He relates different forms of marriages to different stages of social progress with varying rates in different parts of India. *Brahma*, the best form of marriage indicates an advanced stage of social progress, *Daiva*, a stage of great sacrifices, and *Arsha*, a pastoral society.[81] The fact that bridegroom is a suitor, an applicant for the bride's hand, that distinguishes *Prajapatya* form from the *Brahma*, and makes it inferior to the latter, in which the bridegroom is voluntarily invited by the father to accept the bride.[82]

Being an avowed sale of bribe for a pecuniary consideration or bribe-price, Asura form is the ceremony of *Asuras*, or the aboriginal non-Aryan tribes of India. It marks a very low state of society.[83] The *Gandharva* form depending on the mutual desire of contracting parties is permitted to military class and resembles Gretna Green or runaway marriages of English law.[84] The *Rakshasa* form (the bloody seizure of a maiden by force) which is either a relic of barbarous age or an existing practice of lawless tribes illustrates the value of ancient law as a record of the past.[85] The last and basest form of marriage *Paisacha* (Embracing sleeping or drunken damsel) seems to have been enumerated as a form of marriage, only out of regard for the honour of the unfortunate damsel.[86] So Macnghten's view (*Principles of Hindu Law* 3rd ed., 60) that *Paisacha* form is an instance in which fraud is legalised by the Hindu law gets rejected by Banerjee.

Banerjee has studied the mode of contracting marriage and ceremonies into two parts: the betrothment and the nuptial fire and highlighted their importance foı publicity, validity and intentional purity. He then analyses the legal consequences of Hindu marriage under four heads:[87]

1. Those relating to the persons of the parties or the rights of husband and wife over the person of each other.
2. Those relating to their personal capacity.
3. Those relating to their property.
4. Those relating to their offspring.

He observes that duties of the husband and wife are reciprocal, but perfect equality of rights in the married couple has never yet been allowed by any system of law.[88] Banerjee, like Henry Maine, accepts that as a rule, in the Hindu law, the state of women is one of perpetual tutelage; but he also adds that it (Hindu Law) is far more equitable towards the female sex than most systems.[89]

Banerjee discusses the dissolution of marriage – widowhood – in the Hindu law. In his opinion, Sir T. Strange's view that the right of divorce in the Hindu law is marital only is not correct. He asserts,

> 'If by divorce is meant dissolution of marriage, it is not obtainable even by the husband, for, according to *Manu* (ix, 46), a wife can never be released from her husband; and if by the right of divorce is meant the right of either spouse to desert or to live separate from the other, such right belongs under certain circumstances, to the wife as well as to the husband.'[90]

He remarks that though Hindu law imposes many austere duties upon the widow who with all her hardships is the result of unequal legislation, also allows her important rights, for example, the right to maintenance, and others.[91]

Banerjee does not omit the consideration of different kinds of qualification parameters for parties to marriage according to Hindu law. He finds that minors, idiots and lunatics, the deaf and dumb, persons incurably diseased, impotent persons are incompetent to marry. The woman belonging to same *Gotra* or to a different caste is prohibited to be taken in marriage. He comments that above rules of Hindu law embody such prohibitions to an extent which is sufficient for all practical purposes.[92] For example, prohibition on *sapind* marriage can be mentioned. The Hindus in those days lived in joint families and under the same roof for generations together; and their remote collaterals were brought into contact in the same way as the brothers and sisters in modern society. The prohibition of marriage between remote collaterals was not, therefore, as unnecessary as it may now seem to be.[93]

From the above description, a complex nature of marital laws of Hindus appears, but surprisingly there was scarcity of cases about Hindu marriage before the presidencies' courts in British India. Banerjee attributes this trend to the sacramental character of marriage in Hindu law. He says, 'Owing to this, Hindus are so careful to observe the rules concerning marriage and to avoid error, unless it be on the safe side, and so strong is their disinclination to question the validity of marriage in any case, that disputes concerning this topic seldom arise for judicial determination.'[94]

D.F. Mulla is a renowned legal historian of British India who has studied the Hindu marriage law in the light of concerning court-decisions in his book *Principles of Hindu Law* (1st ed., 1912). He holds the view that marriage according to Hindu law is a holy union for the performance of religious duties. It is not a contract; the mere fact, that a marriage was brought about during the minority of either party thereto, does not render the marriage invalid.[95] Commenting on the different forms of marriages, he rejects the notion that regards *Gandharva* marriage as an euphemism for concubinage. He says, 'This view is based on a total misconception of the leading texts of *Smritis*. It may be noted that the essential marriage ceremonies are as much a requisite part of this form of marriage (*Gandharva*) as of any other unless it is shown that some modification of those ceremonies has been introduced by custom in any particular community or caste.'[96]

Dwarka Nath Mitter's *The Position of Women in Hindu Law* (1913) is a comprehensive study of the marital laws of the

Hindus and can be regarded to some extent as a representative of nationalist approach. He rejects the notions of promiscuity in Indian context and asserts the prevalence of systematic marriage right from the beginning. He, relying on the Vedic *Mantras* and their interpretation by *Mimansa* rule, claims, 'Marriage was an established institution at the very commencement of the Vedic period: we find clear and distinct traces of this institution in the *Rigveda*, which is the earliest *Veda*.'[97] In his opinion, the condition of Vedic society was not of a very primitive description ... but on the other hand hymns betray an advanced stage of civilization. The condition of promiscuity as found in the legend of *Svetaketu* might have prevailed amongst the non-Aryan aborigines, and when they were adopting the institution of marriage from their Aryan conquerors, this legend might have been introduced, and in order to give it an air of authority, it was connected with the name of *Svetaketu*, son of *Uddalak*.[98]

Similarly Mitter has rejected the oft-quoted references to support the existence of polyandry in ancient Indian perspective. In his findings, *Aswins* connected with *Suryya* (daughter of *Sun*) appear elsewhere in their inferior capacity of groomsmen, who, on behalf of *Soma*, sue for the hand of *Suryya* from her father. Further, in *Aitareya Brahmana*, a distinct prohibition against a wife having more than one husband at one time is found.[99] In the *Smritis*, like the Code of *Manu*, no trace of polyandry can be found. The single instance of *Draupadi's* (whose example being Superhuman was not to be followed by human beings) marriage with five husbands cannot support the theory that polyandry was in vogue in ancient India at any time.[100]

Regarding different forms of marriages, Mitter's views are seldom at variance with those of other scholars. He does not support G.D. Banerjee's notion identifying the *Arsha* form with *Asura*. He (Mitter) writes, 'This form of marriage could not be regarded as sale (of *Asura* form), for the cows or oxen given to the bride were constant in number, and in a sale or purchase, the price of the girl would vary, according to her beauty or prettiness.'[101] He adds that the cattle (of the *Arsha* form) were given in fulfilment of the sacred law ... but in the *Asura* form of marriage, wealth was given not in accordance with the injunction of sacred law, but as the price for the bride.[102] But the acceptance of Mitter's interpretations among historians is doubtful, since at a later period, A.S. Altekar again has described the cows and oxen as bride-price and regarded the *Arsh* form as the refined relic of *Asura* form of marriage.[103]

Mitter's views about some prohibited degrees on marriage are almost similar to those of other scholars. For example, he, like G.D. Banerjee, attributes the prohibition on *sagotra* marriage to the joint family system of Hindus.[104] In the Vedic age, marriage of girls after attainment of puberty was the rule. During the period of *Smritis*, the age of eight years was considered the earliest age of marriage. There are passages in the various *Smritis*, to show that, in any case, marriage of girls must take place before puberty. In this regard, Mitter says,

> 'The direction to marry a girl, while she is still an infant, seems to be in the nature of a moral injunction, and the disobedience of this precept does not render the marriage either void or voidable.[105] He further writes, 'It has been said that early marriages is an institution which is peculiar to India. But this is indeed far from the truth. Such marriages were known in England even in Tudor times (1403–1603).'[106]

Mitter analyses the views of Maine, Colebrooke, G.D. Banerjee, and Sir Thomas Strange about the necessity of ceremonies to constitute a valid marriage and arrives at his own conclusion. He finds that the gift and acceptance create a valid marriage, and that the ceremonies following them are necessary, more as evidence of marriage rather than as essential ingredients for constituting it.[107]

Regarding the overall position of women, Mitter summarizes his findings by saying 'A Hindu marriage involves the principle of the wife's subordination to the husband, but it is modified by the infusion of the principle of partnership.'[108]

The historiography of the marital laws of Hindus was greatly enriched by the eminent scholar P.V. Kane's erudite work *History of Dharmasastra* (Five volumes, 1930–62). His views on Hindu marriage rules expressed mainly in Vol. II, part I of his work are almost similar to those of scholars like Mitter.

Kane too rejects the existence of any state of promiscuity and asserts that 'throughout the ages for which literary tradition is available in India, marriage has been highly thought of.'[109] Regarding the much-alleged practice of child marriage, he notes, 'when marriages of girls of tender years took place, they were purely a sacrament. There was no question of consummation which took place only after puberty. Sages condemned intercourse even with one's wife before she attained puberty'[110]. But the good number of widows in ancient as well in modern times seems sufficient to nullify this notion. However, Kane's study of nature and forms of marriage, related prohibitions, ceremonies, effects of marriages and widowhood is well-researched.

Studies on the marriage laws in ancient India were further strengthened by a number of scholars such as Srikant Mishra (*Ancient Hindu Marriage Law and Practice*, 1994) but it was historians like R.S. Sharma and Romila Thapar who introduced new approaches to study the subject. R.S. Sharma, representing the Marxist line of historical research, has viewed early Indian institution of marriage in his *Perspectives in Social and Economic History of Early India*.

He traces the existence of promiscuity in ancient Indian society. Prof. Sharma says, 'Even after the establishment of the institution of marriage, some practices, reminding of the old stage of promiscuity lingered till the time of the *Smritis*, with the result that the lawgivers had to make provision for sons born of intercourse beyond the recognized married connections.'[111] But Sharma finds it difficult to determine the extent and period of the prevalence of such promiscuous relations.[112] Earlier, D.N. Mitter regarded promiscuity as a non-Aryan practice; but Sharma notes, 'We cannot clearly. determine whether this practice was confined to the Aryans or non-Aryans, or to both.'[113] R.S. Sharma's special emphasis is on the study of 'Varna influence on marriage forms and practice'. He analyses the various forms of marriages in relation to the origin and growth of class-society. For instance, he observes that:

> 'the two forms of marriages, the *Asura* in which the importance of women is indicated by the bride-price for her and the

Paisacha which appears like a remnant of a state of promiscuity, all generally recommended for the *Vaisyas* and *Sudras*. Most probably these measures were intended to validate the marriage practices of those tribes who were absorbed as the two lower *Varnas* in ancient society'.[114]

He takes the *Rakshasa* form to be a survival of tribal stage which ceased to be respectable with the stabilization of society. Besides, disputing Jolly's view that *Gandharva* form was privilege of the nobles, he proves it to have been open to all castes.[115]

R.S. Sharma believes that the considerations of caste are introduced in the regulations regarding various aspects of marriages. He highlights the linkages of caste with *Niyoga*, widow-remarriage, monogamy and *sati*-system. He accepts the prevalence of inter-caste marriage but adds that due to some reasons it could not help the cause of social reform much.[116] First, generally these marriages are in the *Anuloma* order: higher caste men marrying lower caste women. Second, the majority of instances (of inter-caste marriages) relate to the marriages between the two higher castes.[117] Thirdly, marriages did not admit lower caste wives into the caste of their higher caste husband. Not only are different ceremonies prescribed for wives belonging to different castes but also the modes of greetings meant for wishing them according to their caste are there.[118]

One of the most controversial issues regarding Hindu marital practices among the historians has been the burning of widow or Sati-system. Sir Henry Maine, reflecting many other imperialist scholars opined that this institution (*Sati*) had its origin in the Brahmanical dislike to the enjoyment of property by women and was intended to combat the ancient rule of Civil law which made her tenant for life in respect of her husband's property.[119] But most Indologists like Colebrooke, Wilson, Jolly and Max Müller do not uphold this view.

Jolly asserts that *Sati* custom is hardly ever mentioned in the whole range of the Vedic literature and *Sutra* works. The principal *Smritis* are silent about *Sati*. Only the later *Smritis: Daksha, Vyasa, Usanas*, etc., offer particular references and descriptions of *Sati*.[120] So he concludes that *Sati* was never a special Brahamanical institution.[121] Majority of Indian historians agreed to Jolly's findings. P.V. Kane notes that Sati was not in historic times a practice imposed by priests or men on unwilling women. It may be that the cases of *Sati* occurred because of the force of popular sentiment.[122] On the basis of his study of numerous literary and epigraphic records, Kane claims the rarity of instances of *Sati*. Its prevalence more in Bengal is attributed by him to the higher rights of succession granted to wives which instigated men to get rid of the widows.[123]

R.S. Sharma has described *Sati* as a typically aristocratic practice confined to the *Kshatriyas*. *Kshatriyas* – comprising rulers and fighters – had the strongest sense of possession and love for a good family name.[124] At another place, he remarked that *sati* system arose not only because of patriarchal, class-divided and property-based society but also due to the deep belief in the *Punya* which a widow was supposed to gain by performing the rite of self-immolation.[125]

From the above survey, covering a vast range of periods, it becomes obvious that different historians have interpreted ancient Indian marital laws in different ways. Which one is correct and which one is not, cannot be decided categorically. Historians often have certain prejudices in one or another form which reflect in their judgements on the past, and this can be seen in the case of modern historiography of ancient Indian marriage law as well. One of the major tendencies among the Europeans has been to view everything including Indian marriage rules in the light of religious framework. Indian writers challenged western assumptions but their nationalist zeal often led them to idealize the Hindu marriage system. For example, D.N. Mitter accepts the commencement of institution of marriage right from the beginning of history and rejects the prevalence of promiscuous relations in Indian context but this seems unsound on historical and sociological parameters. Marxists did a great service to the study of marital regulation by viewing it in the light of socio-economic processes, but too much emphasis on caste considerations led them to undermine spiritual and ideological factors.

In fact there can be no monolithic generalization about the marital laws of ancient Indians, since the concerning legal texts are at great variance in relation to time and space. So, different provisions regarding marriage such as polyandry, monogamy, prohibited degrees, inter-caste marriages, effects of marriage, widowhood and marital ceremonies, found in different texts have to be studied in entire historical perspectives. For example, discourage to *Anuloma* marriages (namely by *Vyasa* and *Usanas*) in post-Gupta period is to be seen in accordance with other contemporary restrictions on socio-economic mobility. Further, any attempt to study the marital laws must be holistic, since significant institutions like marriage involves almost all the factors, be it geographical, social, economic, religious, ideological or any other.

Sonship and Adoption

Ancient Indian legal texts have done elaborate provisions on the type, nature, ceremonies and legal effects of sonship. In respect to time and space, there is a great amount of difference among the *dharmasastrakaras* on the issue of sonship. No less difference is seen among the modern writers who tried to analyse the sonship and adoption laws with their own interpretive models. Therefore in the past about two hundred years, innumerable interpretations pertaining to ancient Indian sonship have emerged.

The German Indologist J. Jolly who did one of the earliest studies on the subject has attached greater significance to the theory of sonship. He writes, 'The twelve kinds of son-ship which to some extent are based on the illicit connections of the mother and for the greater part have nothing to do with the blood-relationship of the son with the father, are probably the most striking feature of the Indian family law.'[126] He opined that the cause of abnormal importance being attached to male issues is to be sought, according to *Smritis* in the offering of sacrifices to the means which depends upon the male issue.[127] He added, 'Yet however originally an economic motive was perhaps a more important factors in it – to get for the family as many powerful workers as possible.'[128]

Jolly sees the impact of *patria potestas* (Patriarchy), which Henry Maine had projected vehemently in ancient Roman and Hindu law, on the notion of adoption. He says, 'The children belong to the husband – the owner of the wife – even through adoption he can take into his *patria potestas* other children out of that of another person.'[129]

Regarding the position of various sons, Jolly observes,

> 'A hierarchy of at least 12 sons has been made among whom each preceding member gets the preference over the succeeding ones in inheritance. The *Aurasa* (legitimate son) is always at the top of the list while the order and nomenclature of the others vary according to particular individual opinions and school traditions.'[130]

Jolly has described different types of sons such as, *Kshetraj* (the son by *Niyoga*), *Putrikaputa* (the son of the daughter), *Paunarbhava* (son of remarried widow), *Kanina* (son of the damsel), *Sahodha* (a son with whom the mother was pregnant even at the time of her marriage), *Gudhaja* (son born of wife's adulterous intercourse) and many adopted sons *(Datta, Dattaka, krita, savayamdatta, apvidha)*, etc.[131] In most of the enumerations of the 12 sons, they are divided into two groups each and only the first six are recognised as heirs and the latter six only as relations but not as heirs to their legal father.[132] Jolly remarks, 'The latter group of six sons reminds us of the modern institution of *Dharmaputra* who as the 'duty son' or the representative of a son has only to offer sacrifices to the manes.'[133]

Jolly tries to notice the impact of the process of social change on the theory of sonship. He writes,

> 'The more the other kinds of sonship fell into desuetude through the advance of morality and increasing prevalence of child marriage, so that they came to be regarded merely as an odious privilege of the *Rishis* of yore, out of vogue in the present day, the more was the theory of adoption improved and was at last developed into one of the most important institutions of Indian law.'[134]

With this, Jolly turned to delineate the ceremonies of adoption (*Dattaka*) and compared it with the relevant modern Indian practices.

Jolly was followed by a number of Western and Indian scholars who pursued the study of sonship and adoption in ancient Hindu law. J.D. Mayne maintained that the idea of several kinds of son emerged due to diverse importance attached to sons and loose nature of sexual relation in ancient period. He says that the principle underlying the recognition of sonship is to be found in the indispensableness of a son to an ancient Aryan householder which would lead to every contrivance being exhausted to procure one, and that the relations between the sexes in early times were such that neither delicacy nor sentiment would stand in the way.[135]

But the Indian scholars like P.N. Sen has criticised Mayne's view. He says, 'It seems to be absurd to suppose that the recognition of all these persons as sons was solely due to the intense desire of an ancient householder to have a son at any caste.'[136] He continues, 'No doubt the customs of adoption and appointment had their origin in the desire to have a male child to perpetuate the lineage and offer funeral oblations, but even then, the practice of appointment was condemned by *Manu* in doubtful terms.'[137] Referring many instances of dignified bachelor people and austerities by chaste women, widows going to celestial region without leaving any issue, as mentioned in legal texts, Sen observes, 'I should like to know where fidelity to the husband is enjoined in stronger terms, and its violation more severely condemned than in the text quoted above.'[138]

P.N. Sen has interpreted the much emphasized notion of *patria potestas* in accordançe with Hindu jurists' belief which maintains that 'between the owners of the land and that of the seed, the crop belongs clearly to the land-owner, for the receptacle is more important than the seed (*Manu*)'.[139] Accordingly, he notes, 'That the husband becomes invested with *patria potestas* over the son of that women although he may not have been the real procreator of the child ...'.[140] Besides, Sen has studied various aspects related with parental relationship in Hindu laws.

P.V. Kane has presented an erudite survey of vast Sanskrit texts on sonship laws. He questions Jolly's view attributing the need of so many sons to sacrificial duty and 'economic motive'.

He comments that the learned writer appears to hold that the *Smritis* regarded all the secondary (except *aurasa*, principal son, all sons are sons are secondary) sons equally competent to confer spiritual benefit and that at one and at the same time a man could have all or most of them as sons. But he (Jolly) is mistaken in both these respects.[141] He (Kane) adds, 'The very definition of *putrikaputra, kshetraj* and *dattaka* given by many of the *smritis* shows that one who has already an *aurasa* son, grandson or great grandson could not have a *putrikaputra*, a *kshetraja* or an adopted son. If the definitions of all the 12 or 13 kinds of sons are carefully analysed, it will be quite apparent that the long list is due to the ancient writers' great *penchant* for divisions and sub-divisions based upon very slight differences of circumstances.[142]

Kane has devoted a full chapter entitled *dattaka* to adoption laws. He finds that the *Sutras* (save *Vashisth Dharmsuta)* and *smritis* contain hardly anything about the *dattaka* except his name or the definitions. The *Mitakshara* does not contain more than a few lines on the *dattaka*. It is only in such late works (belonging to the 17th century and later) like the *Vyavahar Mayukha*, the *Dattakmimansa*, the *Dattakchandrika* that *dattaka* receives an elaborate treatment.[143] Kane has traversed every aspect pertaining to adoption such as eligibility for adopted and people who addopt, object of adoption, the requisites and ceremonies of adoption and results of adoption. Regarding the legal effects on the family-relation by adoption, he states, 'It is clear that the severance from the natural family brought about by adoption is only partial and restricted to *pinda* and *riktha* and connected matters and not complete as stated or assumed in several cases.'[144]

It is to be noted that almost all the legal writers and historians of Hindu law have commented on the sonship and adoption laws. But the major points of historiographical debate are as mentioned above. Despite many commendable provisions on sonship, *Dharmasastras* somewhere reflect prejudices on the basis of caste and gender. For example the sons borne of lower caste wife are not equally entitled to inherit parental property. Similarly, women are debarred from the right to adopt and right to give their son for adoption. This skewed provisions remained as it is for centuries, it is very recently that equitable and women-friendly laws have begun to be framed, one such being Amended Marriage Bill, 2010.

Thus, it has been tried to study the modern interpretations of social legislation in ancient India, under three heads: creation of social order, marital laws and sonship. The last two fall under the broader category of family laws while the first one is about the overall structure of society. From the above survey, there remains no doubt that all the three sections are intimately connected to each other. Creation of social structure is fundamental foundation wherein all other institutions (like marriage, sonship, etc) are shaped. This is why the merits and demerits of social hierarchy are apparently felt in other areas of laws. Accordingly, the historiography of such subjects has to be holistic and comprehensive in nature.

Notes

1. Mill, James., *The History of British India*, Vol. I, p. 126.
2. Ibid., p. 127.
3. Ibid., p. 128.
4. Ibid., p. 129.
5. Ibid., p. 135.
6. Ibid., p. 135.
7. Wilson, H.H., footnotes in James Mill., op. cit., p. 135.
8. Ibid., p. 135.
9. Maine, Sir Henry Sumner, *Ancient Law*, p. 17.
10. ——. *Village Communities in the East and West*, p. 57.
11. Elphinstone, Mountstuart, *The History of India*, ed, Cowell, 9th (ed.), p. 14.
12. Ibid., p. 17.
13. Ibid., p. 17.

14. Senarte, quoted in S.V. Ketkar's *History of Caste in India*, p. 14.
15. Risely. Quoted by Jai Shankar Mishra:, *Prachin Bharat ka Samajik Itihas,* p. 164.
16. Ghurey, G.H., quoted by Jai Shankar Mishra, op. cit., pp. 164–165.
17. Dumont, Louis, quoted in Irfan Habib, *Religion in Indian History*, p. xviii.
18. Lingat, Robert, *The Classical Law India*, p. 32.
19. Senart, quoted in Robert Lingat, op. cit., p. 36.
20. Lingat, Robert, op. cit., p. 36.
21. Ibid., pp. 36–37.
22. Ibid., p. 32.
23. Dutt, R.C., *Early Hindu Civilization*, pp. 6–7.
24. Ibid., p. 7.
25. Ibid., p. 138.
26. Ibid., p. 141.
27. Ibid., p. 142.
28. Ghoshal, U.N., *A History of Indian Political Ideas*, p. 186.
29. Kane, P.V., *History of Dharmasastra*, Vol. II, part I, p. 22.
30. Ibid., p. 28.
31. Ibid., p. 27.
32. Ibid., p. 137.
33. Ibid., p. 51.
34. Ibid., p. 65.
35. Ibid., p. 138.
36. Ibid., p. 164.
37. Ibid., p. 164.
38. Essence of Kane's view, pp. 180–187.
39. Kane, P.V., op. cit., pp. 168–169.
40. Ibid., p. 170.
41. Ibid., pp. 170–171.

42. Sharma, R.S., *Perspectives in Social and Economic History of Early India*, p. 24.
43. Ibid., p. 24.
44. Ibid., p. 25.
45. Ibid., p. 25.
46. Ibid., pp. 29–30.
47. Ibid., p. 30.
48. Ibid., p. 31.
49. Ibid., p. 32.
50. Ibid., pp. 32–33.
51. Ibid., p. 30.
52. Thapar, Romila, *Ancient Indian Social History*, p. 196.
53. Ibid., p. 30.
54. Ibid., p. 30.
55. Ibid., p. 32.
56. Lubbock, Sir John, quoted in G.D. Banerjee., *The Hindu Law of Marriage and Stridhana*, p. 22.
57. Westermarck., quoted in Srikant Mishra., *Ancient Hindu Marriage Law and Practice*, p. 7.
58. Colebrook's *Digest*, Book V, p. 122.
59. Maine, Sir. Henry Sumner., *Ancient Law*, p. 134.
60. Ibid., p. 135.
61. Ibid., p. 135.
62. Ibid., p. 132.
63. Ibid., p. 131.
64. Jolly, Julius, *Hindu Law and Custom*, p. 103.
65. Ibid., p. 103.
66. Ibid., p. 103.
67. Ibid., p. 104.
68. Ibid., p. 106.
69. Ibid., p. 107.
70. Ibid., p. 111.

71. Ibid., p. 113.
72. Ibid., p. 114.
73. Ibid., p. 127.
74. Ibid., p. 137.
75. Ibid., p. 137.
76. Banerjee, G.D. op. Cit., p. 25.
78. Ibid., p. 25.
79. Ibid., p. 30.
80. Ibid., p. 31.
81. Ibid., pp. 80–81.
82. Ibid., p. 82.
83. Ibid., p. 83.
84. Ibid., p. 85.
85. Ibid., p. 86.
86. Ibid., p. 87.
87. Ibid., p. 111.
88. Ibid., p. 115.
89. Ibid., pp. 115–116.
90. Ibid., p. 189.
91. Ibid., p. 206.
92. Ibid., p. 67.
93. Ibid., p. 69.
94. Ibid., p. 31.
95. Mulla, D.F., *Principles of Hindu Law*, p. 463.
96. Ibid., p. 464.
97. Mitter, D.N., *The Position of Women in Hindu Law*, p. 196.
98. Ibid., p. 201.
99. Ibid., pp. 204–205.
100. Ibid., pp. 206–207.
101. Ibid., p. 212.
102. Ibid., p. 213.

103. Altekar, A.S., *The Position of Women in Hindu Civilization*, p. 45.
104. Mitter, D.N., op. cit., pp. 233–234.
105. Ibid., p. 243.
106. Ibid., p. 243.
107. Ibid., p. 271.
108. Ibid., p. 338.
109. Kane, P.V., op. cit., p. 427.
110. Ibid., p. 446.
111. Sharma, R.S., op. cit., p. 38.
112. Ibid., p. 38.
113. Ibid., p. 38.
114. Ibid., p. 50.
115. Ibid., pp. 50–51.
116. Ibid., p. 54.
117. Ibid., p. 58.
118. Ibid., pp. 58–59.
119. Maine, Sir Henry Sumner, quoted in D.N. Mitter, op. cit., p. 356.
120. Jolly, Julius, op. cit., pp. 145–146.
121. Ibid., 146.
122. Kane, P.V., p. 630.
123. Ibid., p. 635.
124. Sharma, R.S., op. cit., pp. 57–58.
125. ——. *Prambhik Bharat ka Arthik Aur Samajik Itihas*, p. 92.
126. Jolly, Julius, op. cit., p. 156.
127. Ibid., p. 156.
128. Ibid., p. 156.
129. Ibid., pp. 156–157.
130. Ibid., p. 157.
131. Ibid., pp. 157–159.

132. Ibid., p. 160.
133. Ibid., p. 160.
134. Ibid., p. 161.
135. Mayne, quoted in P.N. Sen., *The General Principles of Hindu Jurisprudence*, p. 232.
136. Sen, P.N., op. cit., p. 232.
137. Ibid., pp. 232–233.
138. Ibid., pp. 233–234.
139. Ibid., p. 235.
140. Ibid., pp. 234–235.
141. Kane, P.V., *History of Dharmasastra*, Vol. III, p. 648.
142. Ibid., pp. 648–649.
143. Ibid., pp. 663–664.
144. Ibid., pp. 697–698.

4

Proprietary Laws in Ancient India

An Interpretational Insight

Property plays a very significant role in the functioning of a family life. It acts like binding factor among family members owning to its coparcenary features. At the same time it also creates rifts in the family and community in cases of perceived ownership from various claimants which leads to individual ownership. The critical role played by the property prompted the law-givers in ancient India to make provisions on each and every aspects pertaining to property. The history-writing in modern time is equally rich with the commentaries over the proprietary laws of ancient India which can be perused under some major topics: property and ownership, succession and inheritance, women's property rights.

Property and Ownership

The notion of property and ownership finds a very subtle treatment by ancient law-givers of India. Both meaning *svatva* and *svamitva* respectively seem to bear the sense of technical terms not that of usual ones. Property signifies the 'things' and ownership 'person' holding them; but both are mutually indicative. Property is generally divided into two kinds, *sthavara* (immovable, such as land and houses) and *jangama* (movable). On the basis of ownership, property may again be categorized into two classes: joint family property and separate property.

According to *Dharmasastrakars*, the chief sources of property are: succession (*Daya*), gains (in trade), purchase, loans, booty, acquisitions and donations, etc. But about the notion of ownership, its transfer is more elaborately dealt with. Making donations and sales are the two important measures for the transfer of ownership. Such seemingly simple provisions are minutely described, and vast difference of opinions among law-givers has rendered the subject to a highly complicated one. So is the case with modern historiography of the subject wherein the difference of opinions among historians has led them to different interpretations.

As in case of many other topics, here also James Mill can be taken to begin with. Mill admits that the sources of acquisition, by occupancy, by labour, by contract, by donation, by descent: which are recognised in almost all states of society, are recognised in Hindustan.[1] He observes,

> 'In an age, however, in which the means of detecting fraudulent acquisition, and of proving the good faith of contracts and bargains, are imperfectly known, purchases and sales, made in public, are alone considered valid. Similar circumstances have suggested a similar expedient to the people of Hindustan'.[2] But he adds, 'The right however, conveyed by a bona fide purchase is not among the Hindus carried to that extent, which is found requisite in a commercially and highly civilized society.'[3]

In Mill's opinion, the topic of 'Rescission of sale and purchase' among the 18 titles of Hindu law indicates that 'rude people, little accustomed to take their decisions upon full and mature consideration' who 'repent their bargains and wish to revoke them'.[4] He, taking the references from the *Code of Manu*, notes, 'A variety of cases are enumerated, in which, if dissatisfied with his bargain, a man may insist upon having it annulled: and in general any sale and purchase of things, not perishable, may be rescinded within ten days, at the will of either of the parties.'[5]

Mill believes that high magnitude of deposits, which are like keeping of property with another person but without the transfer of the ownership signifies a state of insecure society. He remarks,

'In a rude society, in which there is little or no security, and in which the means of concealing valuables is one of the great studies of life, deposits become an object of the great importance. In the Hindu code, other cases of bailment occupy a narrow space: the article of deposits swells alone, to a great size, and forms an object of considerable intricacy and detail.'[6]

Mill disputes Halhed's view that 'the different rates of interest to be paid for the different articles is an institution peculiar to Hindus' and projects its presence among the Jews in the time of Moses as well as in Egypt.[7] Instead, he (Mill) asserts, 'To vary the rates of interest upon the different caste is peculiarity more naturally arising from the unfair and odious distinctions among men created by Hindus'.[8] He has referred many coercive measures for the recovery of loans and thereby commented, 'In the laws related to loans, however, the most remarkable particular is the mode of enforcing payment.'[9]

Mill's above observations on the property and ownership laws of ancient India are entirely in the line of imperialist vision of India's past in general and its law in particular, which have been discussed in previous chapters. He was followed by a number of western historians and scholars who opined on the early Indian legal view of property and ownership. Amongst them Henry Maine stands foremost.

Sir Henry Sumner Maine has first analysed the concept and origin of property in the light of his school of thought, i.e., Historical Jurisprudence or legal evolutionism. He holds the view that the origin of property must be analysed in the light of changing pattern of primitive societies and 'it is concerned not with Individuals, but with Families, not with single human beings, but groups'.[10] He writes, 'It is more than likely that joint ownership, is the really archaic institution, and that the forms of property which will afford us instruction will be those which are associated with the rights of families and of groups of kindred.'[11]

With above hypothetical parameter, Maine sees the dominant prevalence of co-proprietorship in India. He claims, 'The Village Community in India is at once an organised patriarchal society and an assemblage of co-proprietors. The personal relations to each other of the men who compose it are indistinguishably confounded with their proprietary rights ...'.[12] Maine finds that:

> 'the mature Roman law, and modern jurisprudence following in its wake, looks upon co-ownership as an exceptional and momentary condition of the rights of property'[13] .... 'But in India this order of ideas is reversed, and it may be said that separate proprietorship is always on its way to become proprietorship in common.'[14]

But if we examine Main's observation in the light of evidences, it seems brittle, since there is sufficient evidence of separate and private property, along with joint-ownership in both Dharmsastric canons and convention. Secondly, utility of co-ownership is related with the joint family system of Hindus which influenced greater part of Indian social life. However in another book *Village Communities in the East and West* (1913), Maine adopts a sensitive approach and says, 'The first step towards the discovery of new truth on these subjects is to recognise the Indian phenomenon of ownership, exchange, rent, and price as equally, natural, equally respectable, equally interesting, equally worthy of scientific observation, with those of Western Europe.'[15]

Studies on the property and ownership laws were further enriched by German Indologist Julius Jolly. He in his *Hindu Law and Custom* has commented on a wide range of topics related to property and ownership. He holds the view that seizure of an unclaimed property is of particular importance in establishing ownership. For this reason, a person who makes a piece of hollow (the exact mentioned term is 'follow' which seems misspelt) land arable by felling the trees on it, becomes the owner of the soil.[16] Similarly, the hunted deer belongs to him who hits it first; he who hits it later has shot his arrow in vain.[17] This very principle of acquiring ownership as pointed out by Jolly, reminds us of a similar Roman law of occupancy which provides that *res nullius* (things having no owner) are of those who first take possession of them.

Jolly discusses the two opposite camps, namely *Jimutvahana* and *Mitakshara,* representing religious and secular viewpoints respectively on the question of the role of possession in fixing ownership. The question is whether it is *Sastra* or worldly experience that decides the ownership. The school of historical jurisprudence as led by Maine advocates strongly in favour of latter or 'practical inviolability'.[18] But Jolly remarks:

> 'This perception that the true right of ownership may be recognised and established only with the help of science *(Sastra)* had taken root even at an early period in Indian jurisprudence and philosophy but also a reaction set in the *Smritis* that are taken solely from the observation of daily life and after all, the legal rules of *Smritis* like the laws of grammar, merely serve to exhibit and strengthen what is practised at all times and that therefore the right of ownership does not depend upon the science or the sacred law but upon the experience of the world.'[19]

However, Jolly believes, 'It is more important for the historian to arrive at a solution of the question whether communal or private property was the chief form of ownership than to decide whether origin of property was secular or religious.'[20] He surveys various texts and finds the evidences of joint responsibilities and property of villages or joint property such as (pasture land); but also adds, 'On the other hand the fields mostly furnished with hedges appear always to have belonged to individual properties.'[21] Here, Jolly's findings are more balanced and plausible than those of Maine who had stressed ardently on joint-ownership.

Regarding the restriction on usury (which was categorically prohibited for Brahmans), Jolly comments that 'as usury cannot be altogether stopped, it had to be limited as far as possible, and this the *Smritis* attempt to do particularly by rules about the limits of permissible rate of interest and the length of the period for the accumulation of interest'.[22]

Jolly sees religious motives in the laws of debt and its consequent liability for family members. He finds that liability for debts extends over all the members of family (if the debt is for family purpose) but chiefly on the chief of the family and passes over to his heirs, but not up to great-grandsons. He observes, 'The narrower circle of *Sapinda* relations stretches up to the great grandsons and so here too, as in the law of inheritance, the religious motive connected with the funeral sacrifices plays a prominent role.'[23]

Commenting on the guarantee to the creditor – a surety and pledge – Jolly says that a hypothecation is not mentioned in Ancient Indian literature, there is only pledge of property all the same whether it constitutes of immovable or movable properties.[24] He upholds Mill's view and states that the development of the law of 'deposits' is expressive of the universal insecurity of person and property.[25] He also remarks that 'presents' (*dana, upahara*) which are the primary cause of the development of the theory of personal property of women (*stridhana*) contain both religious and worldly implications.[26] Besides, Jolly has also studied many other issues related to property and ownership laws such as boundary laws, commerce, compensation, land grants, documents and forgery, etc.

When the Indian historians began to write roughly from the second half of 19th century, they presented their own standpoint on the property and ownership laws of the early India. P.N. Sen believes that the idea which underlies the conception of ownership (*svamitva*) on the one hand and the conception of property (*svatva*) on the other, is fundamentally the same.[27] He further observes,

> 'The distinction and inter-connection pointed out above between the conceptions of ownership and property is, I need hardly say, fully recognised and explained by Hindu Jurists with their usual analytical subtlety, and they point out that the correct logical way of comprehending them both is to regard the one as the determinant of the other ... (*Nirupya nirupaka bhava*).'[28]

Regarding the famous controversy about recognition of property either by *sastra* or by popular usage (*laukika svatvavada*) which is expounded by *Jimutavahana* and *Vijnnesvara* respectively, Sen argues strongly in favour of the latter. In this context, he critically examines the objections to *Vijnanesvar*'s view. The thief, says Sen, though having control over stolen things 'cannot freely dispose of stolen articles for the fear of detection and consequent punishment.'[29] (It is needless to recall that 'fitness for free disposal' *Yathechch viniryagarhatva* is a necessary element for the definition of property as noted by Srikrishna Tarkalankar). Secondly, asserts Sen, 'it is altogether erroneous to assume that popular usage recognises the thief as the owner of the stolen articles'.[30]

Sen compares Holland's conception of property with that of Hindu jurists and concludes, 'I affirm that in point of logical subtlety and analytical skill they (Hindu Jurists) have scarcely been excelled even by the most modern exponents of Western Jurisprudence.'[31] Dharmasastras have provided various means of acquisition of ownership for various castes.

In Sen's opinion, 'although *Dharmasastras* lay down certain modes of acquiring property as specially appropriate to a particular caste, it is not thereby implied that any contravention of these directions will in any way affect the growth of ownership.'[32] He adds,

> 'for instance, if a Brahmin instead of following the usual avocations of his own caste takes up those of a *Vaisya* and becomes a cultivator, it must not be understood that the produce of his agriculture will not be his own .... The real significance of these rules is that such conduct as leads to a confusion of functions among the several castes is reprehensible unless justified by necessity and ought to be avoided as much as possible.'[33]

Commenting on the *Parigraha* as a specific mode of acquisition of ownership, which is almost identical with the Roman *occupatio* on *res nullius*, Sen observes that this rule had very little practical application in Manu's days when settled ownership was the rule and creation of first ownership in things which had no previous owner was only heard of in ancient times.[34] Sen's equally original approach is reflected in his study of transfer of ownership.

It is a matter of fact that gifts form an important type of transfer of ownership, but it's controversial whether the donor *(data)* who divests himself of the ownership can at the same time invest the donee (*grahita*) with ownership without his (latter's) concurrence. *Dayabhaga* provides that the donor's act invests the donee with an 'inchoate ownership' which is either perfected or defeated on the donee either by accepting or refusing to accept the gift; while according to *Mitakshara* school, the donor at his option cannot invest another person with ownership without the consent of latter.[35]

Sen has argued against *Dayabhaga* view, since at the time of donation it is difficult to predict donee's acceptance or refusal. Further, this view involves that the gift is not the sole cause of the transfer, but *svikara pragbhava* (or antecedent absence of acceptance which implies subsequent acceptance).[36] He seems to support the Mitakshara view; however his more emphasis is on the 'amount of logical subtlety these Hindu jurists brought to bear upon discussions of this kind.'[37]

Earlier Mayne had observed that few propositions had been laid down with more confidence than the doctrine that under Hindu law 'a gift is invalid without possession (or corporal acceptance).[38] But possession is not possible where immovable property such as land is to be gifted. Sen examines Mayne's view in the light of *Mitakshara* which has provided three kinds of acceptance – mental, verbal and corporal – to make a gift complete. He writes,

> 'In the opinion of *Vijnaneswara*, delivery of possession was not absolutely essential to constitute a valid gift, but it is necessary to remember that a gift unaccompanied by possession is of very risky kind, because, in a case of conflict between two apparent titles, in the absence of any evidence to the contrary, that which is accompanied by possession must prevail.'[39]

In respect to the law of sale, Sen defends the provision on rescission of sale which has been criticized by James Mill terming it as an indicative of 'immature consideration' of 'rude people'. Sen remarks, 'Commercialism need not be the sole guiding principle of a community and an actual hardship should be relieved in so far as it can be done without unjustly entailing equal or greater injury to others.'[40] He continues 'It is therefore highly interesting to find that the Hindu law attempted to reconcile the interest of private purchasers with the interest of trade by laying down certain rules which ... provided some protection against being entrapped into and held fast by hasty and inconsiderate bargains.'[41] Similarly, Sen has discussed various opinions of Hindu jurists on the Law of Prescription (the effect of long possession without any opposition from the true owner), Pledge and Bailment, etc. He, rejecting Jolly who had claimed the absence of hypothecation (a form of mortgage where a borrower pledges collateral to secure a debt), says 'The system of hypothecating property without delivering possession of it to the creditor was prevalent in Bengal at least from the time of Sena Kings.'[42]

Sen was followed by a number of Indian scholars and legal historians who pursued the study of property and ownership laws of ancient India. Among them P.V. Kane is worth special mentioning. Kane has delineated various aspects of the property and ownership in the third volume published in 1946 of his major work *History of Dharmasastra*. Kane's order and heads of related study is in accordance with the ancient division of law. Regarding *Bhukti* or possession, he observes, 'Delivery of possession was the principal mode of transferring ownership in ancient times in almost all systems of jurisprudence and so possession was given great weight as evidence of ownership.'[43]

Kane, on the issue of inference of title from long possession (law of prescription) says that ancient Hindu lawyers put down the tendency to usurp another's property and placed many obstacles in the way of wrongful possession.[44]

James Mill earlier has condemned the coercive measures of Hindu law for the recovery of loans. But Kane, quoting various texts, asserts, 'As compared with the harsh legislation against debtors in most ancient and medieval systems of jurisprudence, the rules (for recovery of loans) laid down by *Smritis* are very mild and humane.'[45] Kane disputes Jolly's view also which had maintained that great grand-sons are not liable to pay debts contracted by his great grand-father. He (Kane) proclaims, 'Dr Jolly is under some misapprehension since *Mitakshara* in two places deals with this matter and expressly states that great-grandson is liable to pay debts contracted by his great-grandfather if he has taken ancestral estate but not otherwise.'[46] Kane's many other findings and conclusions on the property and ownership laws are almost similar to those of Sen's.

The other historians and scholars who enriched historiography of the different aspects of property and ownership laws are many in number. Among them, G.N. Jha (*Hindu Law in its Sources*, Allahabad, 1930) and N.C. Sengupta (*Evolution of Ancient Indian Law*, Culcutta, 1953) have studied the concept of surety ship (*pratibhavyam*) in classical Hindu law. Among some books written in Hindi, *Prachin Hindu Vidhi*, 1981 (by Dr Achchey Lal), has described major issues and opinions about property and ownership while *Prachin Bhartiya Arthik Vichar*, 1981 (by Dr Ramnaresh Tripathi), presents a historical survey of economic thought of early India including the idea of property as found in *Sutra* and *Smriti* texts. Historians like R.S. Sharma, owing allegiance to Marxist ideology, initiated materialistic approaches to perceive issues of property and ownership in the light of 'economic determinism'.

R.S. Sharma's *Material Culture and Social Formations in Ancient India* (Delhi, 1985) runs candidly along Marxist line of historical research. Herein, he studies the origin and growth of property. He believes that transition from Rig Vedic pastoral state to cultivation promoted settled life and even cattle-rearing presupposed some sedentary living. All this created an appropriate climate for developing the institution of property.[47] He observes, 'According to linguisticists there are no clear terms for individual property in Indo-European languages. The sense of possession however is indicated by the word '*sva*': one's own.'[48] Despite various references such as, *pana*, *hiranya*, *urvara*, etc. it is difficult to accept the prevalence of individual property. In this state (Rig Vedic period) there must have been the collective ownership of *Gotra* over land.[49]

It is to be noted that inspired by Fredrick Engels' *The Origin of the Family, Private Property and the State*, R.S. Sharma sees the 'vital connection between the existence of these institutions (including class/caste) and the rise of state.'[50] Accordingly, the emergence of institution of private property in Buddhist era, marked by use of iron technology and surplus production, is one of his major assumptions.

Sharma has studied the subject of 'usury' or lending money which is a source of property, as found in vast legal texts. His views regarding the different rates for different *varnas* are almost similar to those of James Mill's. He notes, 'The difference in rates of interest according to the *varnas* might be explained on the ground of the helplessness of the member of the lower orders whose economic position was generally worse than that of higher *varnas*.'[51] Gifts form an important source of property and in this respect Sharma's analytical study of land grants as a mode of transfer of ownership is commendable.

With this survey of modern interpretations, it becomes overt that property and ownership laws like many other subjects have underwent different perceptions in the varied historiography of long period. Initially imperialist historians like James Mill and Maine condemned every concerning provision including better ones; similarly, nationalists like P.N. Sen not only appeared to idealise Hindu view of property and ownership but also declared it superior to other ancient and modern European counterparts. Such sweeping generalisations often lead to misconception about a historical theme. So a deeper, balanced and comprehensive interpretative model, as applied by J.D.M. Derrett is required to approach the various aspects of property and ownership laws of ancient India.

The postcolonial British Indologist Derrett has published two articles (among many others) entitled 'The Suretyship in India: Classical Law and its Aftermath' and 'An Indian Contribution to the Study of Property' in his *Essays in Classical and Modern Hindu Law* Vol. I (1976, Leiden). In both the articles, he displays his best access to original Sanskrit texts, acquaintance with similar modern concepts, critical approach to available studies and perhaps unbiased conclusions as well. For example, he remarks, 'The best studies of property as a concept (as distinct from the questions whether private property existed in ancient civilizations, whether certain persons ought to own particular kinds of objects, or what are the conditions subject to which owned objects may be used and transferred to other owners or users) have been written by Indians'.[52] He laments the ignorance of 'excellence of the (ancient) discussion' (on property) among modern Western and Indian jurists and attributes this condition to the falling study of *Nyaya* (logic) in universities.[53]

Succession and Inheritance

The law of succession and inheritance stands for the partition of ancestral property of a joint family among its members. Joint property in Hindu legal text is termed as *Daya* or *Riktha* and its partition as *Dayabhaga* or *Rikthaharana*. In this area of law, the most important texts are *Mitaksharar* by Vijnanesvara and *Dayabhaga* by Jimutavavahana, which have been determining the partition of joint property among Hindus for about the thousand years. The basic difference between the two texts or schools (which is due to the different interpretation of the term *sapinda*) lies in manner through which a son inherits ancestral property from his father. *Mitakshara* proposes the doctrine of acquisition of property by birth (*janmsvatvavada*) while *Dayabhaga* believes in the doctrine of acquisition of ownership upon the demise of the last owner (*uparmasvatvavada*).

Since the amount and nature of succession affects the every aspects of social life, it has been the keen area of inquiry among the historians right from the beginning of modern historiography. During 1797–98, H.T. Colebrooke produced *A Digest of Hindu Law on Contracts and Succession* which was actually the English translation of Indian law books on similar subjects. Real significance of such works was in the fact that they proved to be the basic source material for further studies on laws of succession. But as in many other realms, here also it was James Mill who set the tone and temper of early historiography often termed as 'imperialist' writing.

James Mill studies inheritance as an act where the property passes from one owner to another, without any return.[54] He viewed the father rather as the head of a number of partners, than the sole proprietor and then remarked, 'The laws of inheritance of Hindus are almost entirely founded upon this patriarchal arrangement.'[55] Mill is hypercritical while commenting on the qualification and disqualification for the sons to inherit property. Regarding the law which says that the son who is distinguished by science (knowledge) and good conduct shall take a greater share than the rest, he comments,

> 'These clauses are an example of that vagueness and ambiguity, the source of endless dispute, which distinguishes the laws of all ignorant people, and which forms a most remarkable feature in those of Hindustan. What is the criterion to ascertain that superiority in science and virtue, which determines the share of brothers in the division of the paternal estate? Or who is to be the judge?'[56]

Mill further points out 'inconsistency' and 'direct contradiction' in succession rules of Hindus. He says that it is declared that on the failure of natural heirs, lawful heirs are 'pure Brahmans' but yet it is added in the next clause that the wealth of other classes (except Brahmans), on the failure of all heirs, the king may take.[57] But as Wilson himself has clarified in footnotes that there is no contradiction, since the first text relates to the property of Brahmans, but the wealth of other classes (in case of heirlessness) shall be taken by the king alone.[58]

Mill believes that the idea of joint interest in the property of the family established the right of succession in the children, but also served to exclude the right of devising by will.[59] He writes, 'As the property belonged to the parent in common only with his offspring, it could not be regarded as just, that he should have the power of giving it away from them after his death.'[60] He finds no prevalence of possession by testament in Hindu law. In his opinion, 'The Hindus have through all ages, remained in a state of society too near the simplicity and rudeness of the most ancient times, to have stretched their ideas of property so far. The power of disposing of a man's possessions by testament is altogether unknown to their laws.'[61]

Mill's above-mentioned assumptions, though disputable and are at variance with those of Indologists like Halhed and Wilson, went on to be taken as the cliché by many imperialist historians and colonial administrators. Sir Henry Sumner Maine, taking clue from Roman law, defines inheritance as 'a succession to the entire legal position of a deceased man'.[62] The notion was that though the physical person of the deceased had perished, his legal personality survived and descended unimpaired on his heir or co-heirs, in whom his identity was continued.[63]

Since, most western historians including Maine perceive the overbearing influence of religion on Hindu law; consequently the religious elements have been projected in the laws of succession as well. Maine observes,

> 'Among the Hindus, the right to inherit a dead man's property is exactly co-extensive with the duty of performing his obsequies. If the rites are not properly performed or not performed by the proper person, no relation is considered as established between the deceased and anybody surviving him; the Law of Succession does not apply, and nobody can inherit the property.'[64]

Maine's perception is close to the laws of *Dayabhaga* School which had explained the term '*pinda*' as rice ball offered at the *pravana shradha* ceremony on the death of the ancestor. Whoever (mostly sons) performed this rite was *sapinda* and thus heir to ancestor's property. But this was prevalent only in Bengal and Assam. The rest and greater part of the country was governed by *Mitakshara* school which, by explaining the *sapinda* as those having the part of body, established son's right to inherit on the basis of his birth. It is interesting to note that Maine himself seems to have admitted this interpretation in the next chapter in same book. He notes, 'Among the Hindoos, the instant a son is born, he acquired a vested right in his father's property, which cannot be sold without recognition of his joint-ownership. On the son's attaining full age, he can sometimes compel a partition of the estate, even against the consent of the partent.'[65]

Maine strongly asserts that 'to the Romans belongs pre-eminently the credit of inventing the will, the institution which, next to the contract, has exercised the greatest influence in transforming human society.[66] Like Mill, he too doubts the existence of wills in Indian context. He says, 'In Hindoo law there is no such things as a true Will. The place filled by Wills is occupied by Adoptions. We can now see the relation of Testamentary Power to the Faculty of Adoption.'[67]

German Indologist Julius Jolly has studied the laws of heirship along with those of partition. In his opinion, laws of partition especially the items of divisible property mentioned reveal a society of agriculturists as well as of industrials.[68] Besides, he sees the patriarchal influence in the laws of partition. He remarks, 'In a partition taken up by the father the *patria potestas* too of course came into consideration which finds significant expression in the rule of *Harita*. Even the later authors such as *Yajnavalkya, Narada* and *Brihaspati* recognise the absolute power of the father to determine the portions of the sons as he chooses.'[69]

It is generally established in *Smriti* laws that family members suffering from serious physical or spiritual melodies are excluded from inheritance. They could claim only maintenance unless being excommunicated (*patita*). Their exoneration is viewed by Jolly as a mean to benefit Brahmans. He comments, 'However, the *Patita* may regain his position in the caste by performing the prescribed penances and thus the ample grounds for excommunication probably, on the whole, served only to bring profit to the Brahmans by means of the penances prescribed by them'.[70]

In respect to the Law of Succession, Jolly appears opposite to the views of Maine who identified the right to inherit with performing obsequies. Jolly observes, 'It is an exaggeration to consider the law of inheritance to be merely spiritual law in which the performance of the usual funeral sacrifices is rewarded with the claim of inheritance'.[71] He further says, 'Of course in most cases the two coincide, yet however *Pindas* are given, for instance, also to the three female ascendants and three *Matamahas*, i.e., the father of the mother and his two male ascendants, although the offerer of the *Pinda* does not inherit the property of these relations.'[72]

But explaining the term *sapinda* in respect to the sequence of heirs, Jolly admits its vicinity with obsequies. He notes, 'After the sons, come the sons of the sons and after them their sons; the three descendants and the ascendants along with the testator form the close body of *Sapinda* relatives which illustrates the connection of the funeral ceremony with the law of inheritance.'[73]

Jolly finds that female members are generally excluded from inheritance by the ancient authors. Though widow's right of inheritance is recognised in the later *Smritis*, but it is subjected to certain conditions, mainly her chastity.[74]

Jolly deliberates very minutely on the law of reversion which provides that there being no relation to inherit; the property reverts to the king. He explains this rule in the light of some 'uncertain' inheritance rules and rarity of partition. He states, 'Perhaps the uncertainty of the *Smriti* rules about the right of inheritance of distant relations is to be attributed to this law of reversion to the king, and in part certainly also to the fact that partitions were rare in ancient times, for, in undivided families, if male descendants were lacking, the relations living with the owner on the joint property were to inherit and as the result of the catholicity of Indian law with regard to the law of the sonship, such cases were not all too frequent in which no son of one kind or another could be found.'[75]

Here, in this long quotation, a self-contradiction is apparently evident. At one side, Jolly sees the 'uncertainty' as regards the distant relatives' right to inherit, but on the other hand, accepts 'relations living with the owner were to inherit' and influence of 'sonship' which pre-empted the frequency of partition. Logically, rarity of partition indicates certainty of rules.

But unlike Mill, Jolly does not miss to notice that law of reversion does not apply to Brahmans whose heirless property is to go to 'spiritual teacher' pupil, or to the 'learned Brahmans'.[76] He holds the view that complete system of successive heir (after the sons and grandsons, etc) developed only by the medieval jurists but they are marked by wide differences among them particularly in connection with the position and rights of women.[77]

Among the Indian writers of the Hindu law on succession and inheritance, P.N. Sen can be discussed first. He in his *The General Principles of Hindu Jurisprudence* (1918), which indeed is the collection of his *Tagore Law Lectures*, first analyses the differences between *Dayabhaga* and *Mitakshara* Schools on inheritance rules. He observes that distinction between unobstructed (*apratibandha*) and obstructed (*sapratibandha*) heritage (*Daya*) as explained in *Mitakshara* has no place in the doctrine of *Dayabhaga* School, for according to it, neither the son nor any other kinsman acquires any title by birth.[78] 'Even the succession of the son' says Sen 'is liable to be obstructed by the survival of the father; thus the result is, that if you choose to employ the expression 'succession' under the *Dayabhaga* School, it must always be regarded as 'liable to obstruction' (*Sapratibandh*).'[79]

The various types of father's property and son's right over them (as regards *Mitakshara* rules) are points of debate among scholars. Earlier Maine had maintained that son's right by birth is limited only to ancestral property which is inheritance of a direct male ancestor but where the father has inherited from a collateral relation, as for instance, from brother, nephew, cousin, it is not ancestral property. Consequently, his own descendants are not coparceners with him.[80] But Sen rejects this and remarks, 'The right which a son acquires by birth in father's property is not limited to ancestral property alone, but extends over the entire property of his father (such as self-acquired also), although the extent of right is not everywhere the same but depends on the nature of property.'[81]

Dayabhaga acknowledges no such distinction by holding that father in his life time is the absolute owner of all his property whether ancestral or self-acquired. But Sen, relying on some references in *Dayabhaga* – like 'a father ... has equal ownership with his sons in the paternal grand-father's estate', sees sons' interest in ancestral property. He writes, 'From these and other passages it is perfectly clear that although *Jimutvahan*a repudiated the theory that property arose from birth, he allowed to the sons at least so much interest in ancestral property as would place a restraint upon the unlimited discretion of the father in distributing that property, if he, at his option, chose to distribute it.'[82]

Afterwards, Sen discusses the difference between *Dayabhaga* and *Mitakshara* on the issue of partition. He observes that according to the *Dayabhaga*, each of the undivided coparceners has ownership, not over the entire joint property, but only over particular portions and partition ascertains it by specifically allotting several portions to the several coparceners. This doctrine is therefore known as *Pradeshik svatvavada* or the theory of ownership in a part.[83]

But according to *Mitakshara* 'partition is the adjustment of diverse rights regarding the whole, by distributing them particular portions of the aggregate'.[84] The result is that each co-owner is deemed to be the owner of the whole; in the same manner as other co-owners are also owners of the whole, the ownership of one without excluding the co-ownership of the others. This view is known as the *Samudayika Svatvavada* or the doctrine of ownership in the whole.[85]

The logical consequence of diverse conception of co-ownership in an undivided property and partition has its bearing on the power of alienation by a co-parcener. Therefore, according to the strict *Mitakshara* doctrine, an undivided co-parcener has no right to alienate any portion of the joint property without the concurrence of the others.[86] But conversely, it is open to a *Dayabhaga* co-parcener to transfer his own share in the joint property (since he owns a part), and such a transfer would be valid even without the concurrence of other co-parceners who cannot legitimately interdict an alienation of what is not their own.[87]

Sen analyses the difference between *Dayabhaga* and *Mitakshara* schools regarding the relative position of agnates (relations connected through males) and cognates (relations through a female) in the order of succession. He summarizes his study thus,

> 'By the application of the doctrine of spiritual benefit, as interpreted by him, *Jimutavahana* makes room for a number of cognates to succeed even in preference to many agnates, while, according to the *Mitakshara*, none of them excepting the daughter's son of the deceased owner, would have any place until all the agnates however remote, are completely exhausted.'[88]

It is generally assumed that the *Mitakshara* law of succession is based on the principle of propinquity but peculiar favour given to daughter's son is an exception to this rule. In this regard Sen accepts Mayne's 'plausible' explanation. Mr Mayne had suggested that appointing daughter to raise up issue for father was an old practice which later became obsolete, 'but the fact of nearness of the daughter and daughter's son remained, and their natural claim to succession on the ground of mere consanguinity recommended itself for general acceptance'.[89]

In Bengal, *Dayabhaga* innovated the altered course of succession by abandoning the 'almost unqualified preference' given to agnates and by giving better position to certain members of cognates. Sen admits the role of religious efficacy but refutes Mayne's notion of the 'influence of Brahmanism' behind this innovation. Here Sen supports Gopalchandra Sirkar's interpretation that 'the doctrine appears to have been introduced by the author of the *Dayabhaga* as a mere pretext for assigning in the order of succession a higher position to some dear and near cognates who, under the *Mitakshara*, are all postponed even to the most distant agnates'.[90]

The principle of exclusion of females from the succession, which is common to both the schools is attributed by Sen to the 'position of a female in the organization of the ancient Aryan society,' marked by 'life-long dependence.[91] Besides, in his opinion, 'principle that succession can never remain in abeyance' is not a principle founded upon any special text, but is a logical deduction from the conception of succession (in Hindu law).[92]

Thus it is Sen who not only applied the holistic approach to study the law of succession and inheritance, but also analysed the guiding principle behind particular conception. His unambiguous acceptance of females' exclusion from inheritance owing to 'life-long dependence' bespeaks his comparatively balanced approach to history. Afterwards, P.V. Kane, among many others, strengthened the historiography of old Hindu law of succession. He, in the Vol. III of his *History of Dharmasastra* studies this topic in two chapters entitled, 'Dayabhaga' and 'Order of Succession after the Son'.

Kane summarizes the difference between *Dayabhaga* and *Mitakshara* schools in four main points: 1. The *Dayabhaga* denies the theory that property is by birth, while the *Mitakshara* accepts it; 2. *Dayabhaga* lays down that the right to inherit and order of heirs is determined by the principle of religious efficacy, while the *Mitakshara* school holds that blood relationship is the governing factor in this matter; 3. *Dayabhaga* holds that members of a joint family hold their shares in quasi-severalty and can dispose of them even when there is no partition by metes and bounds; 4. *Dayabhaga* holds that even in undivided family the widow succeeds to her husband's share on his death without male issue, while the *Mitakshara* School holds that she does not do so.[93]

The divergent law of succession in Bengal especially in respect to women under *Dayabhaga* has been a puzzle to explain. Justice Saradacharan Mitra attributed it to deltaic character, maritime activities and influence of Buddhistic tantras, all present in Bengal from early medieval period.[94] But Kane, citing availability of these factors in areas other than Bengal, rejects this theory and concludes, 'It is best to admit that no satisfactory explanation can be given of the peculiar doctrines of the *Dayabhaga*. They have an indigenous and independent origin and growth'.[95]

Kane studies the partition under four heads: (1) the time of partition; (2) the property liable to partition; (3) the mode of partition; and (4) the persons entitled to partition. He quotes many references from Rig Veda and other Vedic sources, showing the division of father's property among sons and asserts, 'Dr Jolly's remark that ... in the earliest period of Indian Law, partition of property was an entirely unknown proceedings goes too far and is not fully warranted by Vedic texts.'[96] In his view, recognition of *Vidyadhana* (gains of learning) as a separate property by *Sutras* was 'the first inroad on the conception that earnings of all in the family belonged to the head of the family'.[97]

Commenting on the law of primogeniture and special share for the eldest son, Kane observes, 'Almost all the *sutras* and *smritis* prescribe the rule of equal division among the sons of the wives of the same class as the father. But some of these (like *Manu*) no doubt refer to the special share or provision given to the eldest (called *uddhara*).'[98] He also notes that from certain passages when construed literally (such as *Yajnyavalkya* II, 116,

Narad, Dayabhaga, 15), it appears that early Indian father often distributed the ancestral wealth among his sons just as he pleased .... The eldest son has received special treatment in all ages down to modern times.[99]

It is to be noted that *Dayabhaga* gives a peculiar meaning to the word *Sapinda* by including it in many cognates like sister's son who literally is not a *gotraja.* This remoulding of the technical terms had its reflections on the order of heirs. Kane in this regard observes, 'The *Dayabhaga* thus gives the go-by to the text of *Yajnavalkya* and shuffles in several cognates as very near heirs. The *Dayabhaga* regards *Manu* IX. 186–187 as the crucial text and *Yajnavalkya* II. 135–36 as only secondary.'[100]

Kane's study of other related topics such as, coparcenary and joint family, disqualification to succession, brothers and their sons as heir, *shradhas* and inheritance, propositions about religious benefit, *gotraja* succession, etc., are based on the highly erudite survey of vast Sanskrit texts. If P.N. Sen is credited to have explored the implicit conceptual framework of Hindu inheritance law, it is Kane who enriched the comprehensive research on the every related issue whether major or minor.

Beside them, there are many other historians and writers on Hindu law (both Indian and foreigner) who studied succession and inheritance rules of *Dharmasastras,* such as, I.S. Pawate (*Daya-Vinhaga: Or the Individualization of the Communal Property and the Communalization of Individual Proprty in the Mitakshara Law,* 1945, Dharwar), Sontheimer (*The Joint Hindu Family: Its Evolution as a Legal Institrution,* 1977, Delhi), B.N. Mani (*Laws of Dharmasastra* 1989, Delhi) among many others. It is noticeable that jurists and lawyers writing on the modern Hindu law, mainly on Hindu Succession Act, 1956., have also commented to some extent about the concerning classical law as a background. In this category, P.C. Goyal's *Effects of Hindu Succession Act, 1956, on the Direct Taxation of Mitakshara Hindus* (Allahabad, 1978) can be mentioned. Consequently, modern historiography of the subject went enriched, diversified and contemporised.

Women's Property Rights

The position of women in Hindu law with special reference to their property rights has always been a much-discussed point in historical studies. The entitlement to property is directly related to the questions of survival and empowerment. So not only historians but also the jurists, sociologists and women organisations have voiced their views on the subject. Consequently, innumerable interpretations of the topic have emerged in about past two hundred years. But almost all of them effuse biases and stereotypes, thereby leaving the objective analysis of women's property rights mainly the *stridhana* an unmet challenge. To serve this purpose, it is necessary first to have a critical assessment of the historiography of the subject.

Initiating the research in India's past in the late 18th century, British Indologists and imperialist historians penned about women's property rights in ancient India. James Mill, who laid down the basic imperialist assumptions about the society, polity, religion and law of India, observes that daughters are debarred from a share in the inheritance of their fathers.[101] He says that 'the woman indeed, among the Hindus, is so restricted in the means of acquiring property, that she is almost excluded from its rights.'[102] Mill regards some cases where a little property is given to a woman as 'exceptions'. Referring to the lines from the *Laws of Manu* of Colebrooke's Digest, he opines that if women die without issue, their property falls to their husband or to their parents, and is subject to nearly the same rules of collateral succession as are established in regard to the property of males.[103]

After Mill, his follower Sir Henry Maine who was the scholar of Historical Jurisprudence School studied ancient Indian women's property rights in detail. About the position of women in general, Maine sees the strict prevalence of Roman institution of 'perpetual tutelage' which made the women subject to their male relative as guardian for whole life.[104] Writing the meaning of *stridhana*, he says: 'the settled property of a married woman incapable of alienation by her husband, is well known to the Hindus under the name of *Stridhana*.'[105] Commenting on the definition of stridhana in *Mitakshara*, he remarks that all the property which a woman may have acquired by inheritance, purchase, partition, seizure, or finding, is a comprehensive description of stridhana. It shows that the ancient Hindu law secured to married women, in theory at all events, an even greater degree of proprietary independence than that given to them by the modern English Married Women's property Act.[106]

Maine had rightly perceived that the rule of the *Mitakshara* with regard to *stridhana* is the most liberal one. In his view, this institution of property developed among Hindus much earlier than among Romans; but instead of being matured and improved as it was in the Western society it has been gradually reduced to dimensions and importance far inferior to those which at one time belonged to it.[107] The learned jurist tries to account for the 'amplitude which the Mitakshara assigns to stridhana' from an examination of other bodies of Aryan custom. The result of such an examination led this scholar to hold that the *stridhana* had a pre-historic origin in the bride-price.[108]

After tracing the origin of *stridhana*, Maine observes:

> 'First of all it was property conferred on the wife by the husband at the "nuptial fire" as the sacerdotal Hindoo lawyers express it. Next it came to include what the Romans called the '*dos*', property assigned to the wife at her marriage by her own family. The next stage may very well have been reached only in certain parts of India ... but still there is nothing contrary to the analogies of legal history in the extension of the *Stridhana* until it included all the property of a married woman. The really interesting question is how came the law to retreat after apparently advancing farther than the Middle Roman Law in the proprietary enfranchisement of woman, and what are the causes of the strong hostility of the great majority of Hindoo Lawyers to the text of *Mitakshara*, of which the authority could not be wholly denied?'[109]

Sir Henry Maine shows a characteristic insight into the views of the majority of Hindu lawyers when he says that, putting the author of the *Mitakshara* aside, all the commentators reflect an increasing desire to connect all property with the discharge of sacrificial duties, and with this desire, the reluctance to place property in the hands of women is somehow connected.[110] J. Jolly, who is a great authority on Hindu law, explains this tendency to minimize the women's property rights in the light of expanding description of *stridhana*. He observes that the consideration of males in the line of heirs of *Stridhana* at the time of succession (which is almost inconsistent with *Mitakshara*) indicates an epoch in which the *Stridhana* was developed far beyond mere ornaments and articles of use.[111] It is a matter of fact that initially *stridhana* was mere property obtained by women at her marriage time, but later it began to comprise several types of property including immovable and inherited assets.

J.D. Mayne is also an important name to have expressed his opinion about property rights of women in ancient India. He, like many other writers on Hindu law, comments that women were in very ancient times regarded as merely chattels, that they could be bought and sold, that they were incapable of holding property and that gradually both their status and proprietary position were elevated by the later *Smriti*-writers and commentators.[112] In fact, according to the erstwhile prevailing theory among most western historians, the general principle followed with respect to females in ancient India is that no right can be claimed by them unless it is supported by obvious (male) authority.

Like the western scholars, there are a number of Indians who studied women's property rights in ancient India in a detailed way. Among them Sir Gooroo Dass Banerjee (*The Hindu Law of Marriage and Stridhana*), Dwaraka Nath Mitter (*The Position of Women in Hindu Law*), P.V. Kane (*History of Dharmasastra*, Five Volumes) and Bhim Sain Narang (*Concept of Stridhana in Ancient India*) are of great importance. G.D. Banerjee observes that while declaring the 'perpetual tutelage' of women and their general incapacity to hold property, the Hindu law concedes to them the privilege of holding property of certain descriptions with absolute power of disposal. In his words, 'the law of *stridhana* stands, therefore, in favourable contrast with the general spirit of the Hindu law, which in other respects, is no doubt, not very equitable towards women.'[113] In his view Hindus can find some reason for just complacency in this proprietary rights of women as it was absent in any ancient or mediaeval system of law, except the Mahomedan and the later Roman.[114]

Banerjee studies the three aspects related to *Stridhana*: What constitutes *stridhana*; rights of women over it; and order of succession to *Stridhana*. He describes the various definitions and classifications of *Stridhana* according to different sages (like *Manu, Narad, Katyayan,*) commentators and schools (Mitakshara, Dayabhaga) and finds that, 'the term stridhana is not used in simple etymological sense but has a technical meaning.'[115] However, it is to be remembered that Mitakshara and Virmitrodaya apply it etymologically extending the content of *Stridhana*; but women's power of disposal is not same over every variety of it.

Banerjee analyses diverse rules regarding the order of succession to *stridhana* in different schools, and opines that it generally varies depending on the kinds of property and status of women such as daughter, married, widow. Commenting on the law of *vijnanesvara* wherein women's property is succeeded by her daughter, Banerjee says that, 'the sons exclusively take the property of their father; and as a sort of compensation for this, as it were,. the daughters are allowed preference in the order of succession to their mothers' estate'.[116]

Like Banerjee, D.N. Mitter too studies various texts on the women's property rights. He tries to explain and justify some of the imperialist assumptions such as Maine's 'perpetual tutelage'. He says, 'The aim of the text regarding the dependence of Hindu women was to preserve their chastity and to protect them from vice.'[117] He believes that women could hold the property in Vedic period where the theory of perfect equality of men and women is indicated; but they lost this position anterior to the time of Manu who disqualified a wife, a son and a slave for having the property with their own dominion.[118] But Hindu law gradually established the principle of the active proprietary capacity of women by providing and extending the description of *stridhana* to the inherited property (by *Vijnanesvara)*. *Smritis* show a gradual development of the recognized capacity of women for property which may have corresponded in a measure to the successive generations in which the texts were framed.[119]

In the closing lines of the book, Mitter seems disappointed over the Indian Legislature (colonial period) not ready to accept the liberal definition of *stridhana* by *Mitakshara* which he regards as the strongest advocate of the proprietary rights of women.[120]

The research on women's property rights was further enriched by the erudite work of P.V. Kane. He, accepting the *Sayana*'s explanation of '*Vahatu*' as cows and other objects given for pleasing the girl to be married, traces the germs of *stridhana* to the Vedic literature.[121]

Like Banerjee, Kane too studies the various interpretations of *stridhana* by Smriti writers and commentators, and thereby underlines the gradual expansion of the term. He observes that the dominion or the rights of women over *stridhana* depends on three things:

1. The source of acquiring property
2. Women's status at the time of acquisition (i.e., maiden, married or widow)
3. The school of the law which she is governed by

After a perusal of different texts, he finds that the views of *Katyayana* similar to those of *Narad* and *Deval* about the dominion of the women over *Stridhana* are authoritative in all schools of law.[122]

It is a fact that *Katyayana* has provided that the Hindu women during her maidenhood could dispose of her *Stridhana* property of every description at her pleasure, but during widowhood she could not dispose any immovable property given by her husband, while a married women too could dispose of her *stridhana*; but only that kind of property called *saudayika*,(gifts from relations, husband, parents).

Kane, coming to the order of succession to *Stridhana*, finds great differences in texts but one common thing, viz., daughters are preferred to sons, but later it changed and in certain descriptions of *Stridhana*, sons became preferable to daughters.[123] Kane, like J. Jolly, explains this paradigm shift in the light of expanding nature of *Stridhana*. In his words, 'the value of *Stridhana* property became considerable in later times and society which held to the doctrine of the dependence and inferior position of women, could not tolerate the idea that large estates should go to women'.[124]

Kane's passion for gender equality in property rights is reflected in his suggestions for proposed codified Hindu law (which was later passed in 1955 by parliament). In his opinion the law must abolish sex-based distinctions and women must be provided absolute estate, whenever she succeeds to any property.[125]

Apart from *Stridhana*, Kane makes a thorough analysis of the right to maintenance in Hindu law. Quoting the lines from many *Smriti*-texts, he comes to the conclusion that maintenance for certain persons including wife and mother was a legal liability and failure to it could lead to punishment.[126] Unchastity was a disqualification to maintenance; but there are texts, says Kane, which state that widows guilty of adultery are purified by penance and may be restored to all their social privileges (including the right to maintenance). [127]

No study in the historiographical perspective can be complete unless it discusses the Marxist interpretation which views history with the ideological tool of 'historical materialism'. Seeing the requirement of the present topic, R.S. Sharma can be taken up as the representative historian of this school of thought. He believes that woman herself was supposed to be a kind of property.[128] Women came to be considered a movable property since they were to be debarred from immovable property.[129] The provision of *Stridhana* was a very confined idea as it entitled wives only to jewellery and gifts.[130] Prof. Sharma has explained these phenomena in accordance with his proposition of a typical patriarchal society based on the notion of private property.

Among the Indian historians writing on the topic, Bhim Sain Narang too needs to be mentioned. The main importance of his book *Concept of Stridhana in Ancient India* lies in discussing all the issues pertaining to *Stridhana* at one place with full detail. *The Hindu Women's Right to Property* (Roop Lal Chaudhary), *Position of Women in Hindu Civilization* (A.S. Altekar), *Gendering Caste through a Feminist Lens* (Uma Chakravarti), *The Power of Gender and Gender of Power* (Kumkum Roy) among many others provide some insights into the study of women's proprietary position.

The western writers on Hindu law of post-colonial period betray a comparatively more balanced approach as explained in the first chapter. So is the case with the study of women's property rights. Werner F. Menski has studied women's proprietary entitlement with special focus on maintenance law in his recently published book *Hindu Law, Beyond Tradition and Modernity*.

Menski first analyzes the various interpretations of concerning scholars such as R.K. Agrawal, Flavia Agnes, Manmayee Basu and others and then draws his conclusion in the light of pos-modernist legal analysis. He observes that while Hindu women had defined rights and entitlements in principle, men (and often other women) would, in social reality try and restrict or even deny individual women.[131] He draws the attention to the fact that it was not only women but the men also except the head of the household who were underprivileged in proprietary rights in a joint Hindu family system.[132]

After the above discussion, some observations can be made as the part of the assessment of studies on women's property rights. It is obvious that women were entitled more or less to own property of certain description right from the beginning of the Indian law. So assumptions like James Mill's that women were debarred from property rights cannot be accepted. Perhaps Mill's conclusion is part of a broader imperialist vision of India's past which was guided mainly by the notion of the cultural supremacy of the West. It is equally true that the Hindu law concerning the proprietary rights of women was capable of indefinite expansion, as D.N. Mitter and others have shown in the case of *Stridhana*.

So, there are some significant provisions – at least in theory – for women's economic security, but still it is difficult to find any trace of gender equality in proprietary matters in ancient Indian legislation.[133] In addition to exclusion from paternal/ancestral property, there were serious restrictions on disposing *Stridhana*. According to *Dharmasatras*, the sisters were entitled to get one-fourth of their brothers' share on account of their marriages, but it was, as N.N. Bhattachrya writes 'more an expression of moral obligation than of a legal compulsion'.[134] The situation being so, it is necessary to have a very dispassionate and balanced approach while attempting objective historiography of women's property rights in ancient India.

Thus, it has been tried to traverse the modern interpretational insights into the proprietary laws of ancient India. The three heads: 'Property and Ownership'; 'Succession and Inheritance'; and 'Women's Property Rights' chosen for the chapter are needless to say, expressly connected to one another. In a loose sense, the last two are parts of first topic which is general and inclusive in nature. As per Dharmasastric belief, succession is a mode of acquiring ownership and women's property rights evolve out of the fundamental legislation on property and inheritance.

As regards the historiography, western Indologists and Indian writers on Hindu law are in lead. It is interesting to see that despite belief in materialistic interpretation of the history, Marxist study of the early Indian proprietary law is not of that volume. Perhaps Marxists were concerned more with the economic factors and formations than to the technical-legal framework of property. Besides, in Marxist theory everything including proprietary law is 'superstructure' based on basic structure, i.e., mode of production. This notion too would have led them to secondary treatment of legalist approach to the idea of property.

Notes

1. Mill, James. *The History of British India*, Vol. I, p. 159.
2. Ibid., p. 160.

3. Ibid., p. 160.
4. Ibid., p. 161.
5. Ibid., p. 161.
6. Ibid., p. 162.
7. Ibid., p. 165.
8. Ibid., p. 165.
9. Ibid., p. 166.
10. Maine, Henry. *Ancient Law*, p. 229.
11. Ibid., p. 230.
12. Ibid., p. 231.
13. Ibid., P. 232.
14. Ibid., p. 232.
15. ——. *Village Communities in The East and West*, p. 224.
16. Jolly, Julius., *Hindu Law and Custom*, p. 196.
17. Ibid., p. 197.
18. Maine, Henry., *Ancient Law*, p. 228.
19. Jolly, Julius, op. cit., p. 198.
20. Ibid., p. 203.
21. Ibid., p. 204.
22. Ibid., p. 213
23. Ibid., p. 218.
24. Ibid., p. 220.
25. Ibid., p. 224.
26. Ibid., p. 227.
27. Sen, P.N., *The General Principles of Hindu Jurisprudence*, p. 39–40.
28. Ibid., p. 40.
29. Ibid., p. 43.
30. Ibid., pp. 43–44.
31. Ibid., p. 49.
32. Ibid., p. 54.

33. Ibid., pp. 54–55.
34. Ibid., p. 56.
35. Ibid., pp. 67–68.
36. Ibid., p. 68.
37. Ibid., p. 69.
38. Mayne, quoted in P.N. Sen., op. cit., pp. 69–70.
39. Sen, P.N., op. cit., pp. 70–71.
40. Ibid., pp. 96–97.
41. Ibid., p. 97.
42. Ibid., p. 187.
43. Kane, P.V., *History of Dharmasastra* Vol. III, p. 319.
44. Ibid., p. 325.
45. Ibid., P. 441.
46. Ibid., p. 444.
47. Sharma, R.S., *Material Culture and Social Formations in Ancient India*, p. 27.
48. Ibid., p. 27.
49. Ibid., p. 30.
50. ——. *Aspects of Political Ideas and Institutions in Ancient India*, p. 51.
51. ——. *Perspectives in Social and Economic History of Early India*, p. 199.
52. Derrett, J.D.M., *Essays in Classical and Modern Hindu Law*, Vol. I, p. 476.
53. Ibid., p. 477.
54. Mill, James, op. cit., p. 169.
55. Ibid., p. 169.
56. Ibid., pp. 170–171.
57. Ibid., p. 171.
58. Wilson, H.H., footnotes in James Mill, op. cit., p. 171.
59. Mill, James., op. cit., p. 173.
60. Ibid., p. 173.

61. Ibid., pp. 173–174.
62. Maine, Henry Sumner., *Ancient Law*, p. 161.
63. Ibid., p. 161.
64. Ibid., p. 170.
65. Ibid., p. 202.
66. Ibid., p. 172.
67. Ibid., pp. 171–172.
68. Jolly, Julius., op. cit., p. 180.
69. Ibid., pp. 180–181.
70. Ibid., pp. 182–183.
71. Ibid., p. 184.
72. Ibid., p. 184.
73. Ibid., p. 185.
74. Ibid., pp. 186–187.
75. Ibid., p. 189.
76. Ibid., p. 189.
77. Ibid., p. 189.
78. Sen, P.N., op. cit., p. 128.
79. Ibid., pp. 128–129.
80. Mayne, quoted in P.N. Sen, op. cit., p. 129.
81. Sen, P.N., op. cit., p. 130.
82. Ibid., p. 141.
83. Ibid., pp. 145–146.
84. Ibid., p. 145.
85. Ibid., p. 146.
86. Ibid., p. 150.
87. Ibid., p. 154.
88. Ibid., p. 161.
89. Mayne, quoted in P.N. Sen, op. cit., p. 158.
90. Sen, P.N., op. cit., p. 166.
91. Ibid., p. 170.

92. Ibid., p. 173.
93. Kane, P.V., op. cit., p. 558.
94. Sadacharan, Mitra., quoted in P.V. Kane, op. cit., p. 559.
95. Kane, P.V., op. cit., p. 560.
96. Ibid., p. 565.
97. Ibid., p. 578.
98. Ibid., p. 623.
99. Ibid., pp. 623–624.
100. Ibid., pp. 742–743.
101. Mill, James., op. cit., p. 172.
102. Ibid., p. 173.
103. Ibid., pp. 173–174.
104. Maine, Henry, *Ancient Law*, p. 157.
105. Maine, quoted in D.N. Mitter's *The Position of Women in Hindu Law*, p. 644.
106. Ibid., p. 646.
107. Ibid., p. 645.
108. Ibid., p. 644.
109. Ibid., p. 645.
110. Ibid., p. 645.
111. Jolly, Julius, op. cit., p. 192.
112. Mayne, J.D., *Treatise on Hindu Law and Usage* (6th ed.), p. 86.
113. Banerjee, G.D., *The Hindu Law of Marriage and Stridhana*, p. 32.
114. Ibid., p. 32.
115. Ibid., p. 296.
116. Ibid., pp. 356–357.
117. Mitter, D.N., op. cit., p. 123.
118. Ibid., pp. 601–602.
119. Ibid., p. 603.
120. Ibid., p. 650.

121. Kane, P.V., op. cit., p. 770.
122. Ibid., p. 783.
123. Ibid., p. 789.
124. Ibid., p. 789.
125. Ibid., p. 801.
126. Ibid., pp. 803–804.
127. Ibid., p. 807.
128. Sharma, R.S., *Perspectives in Social and Economic History of Early India*, p. 63.
129. Ibid., p. 63.
130. Ibid., p. 63.
131. Menski, Werner F., *Hindu Law: Beyond Tradition and Modernity*, p. 484.
132. Ibid., pp. 485–486.
133. For the elaboration of this point, see Shiva Kant Tiwari., 'Pracheenn Bhartiya Sampattik Vidhayan me Lingeeya Samata ka Yatharthadarsha', published in *Social Ideals and Reality in Ancient India*, RBSA Publishers, Jaipur, 2017.
134. Bhattacharya, N.N., 'Property Rights of Women in Ancient India', published in *Position and Status of Women in Ancient India*, (ed.) by Prof. L.K. Tripathi, Varanasi, 1988.

5

The Laws of State Affairs

Historiographical Perspectives

The state is the concrete form of various set of laws. In ancient India, state was tasked more with holding out the system mainly *Varna* and *Ashram vyavastha* as perceived by law givers. The deviation from *Varna* and *Ashram Dhrama* was the suggestive of period of downfall and state's duty was to restore the same. But the vision of state varies in the changing socio-cultural and material conditions in ancient and early medieval India. This led to the emergence of diverse approaches regarding the origin, nature and functioning of the state in modern historiography.

Origin and Nature of State: Imperialist Historiography

First and foremost notion to reflect in the imperialist vision of state in ancient India is the idea of 'Oriental Despotism'. 'Oriental Despotism' can be traced back to Plato and Aristotle, but it was only when the Mercantilist and the first generation industrial powers acquired colonies in India and other part of Asia that the idea was popularized. Amongst other, it is found in the writings of Adam Smith, Montesquieu, Richard Jones and Hegel, and was propagated by James Mill.

James Mill, the utilitarian thinker who is regarded as the first true historian on India, asserts, 'Among the Hindus, according to the Asiatic model, the government was monarchical, and with the usual exception of religion and its ministers, absolute. No idea of any system of rule, different from the will of the single person, appears to have entered the minds of them or their legislator.'[1] He adds that in the West, government was based on the principles of 'checks and balances' and 'division of power'. The central authority was divided into many departments and each was assigned a specified task. But Mill thinks, the machinery through which the power of the sovereign was exercised in ancient India 'was a contrivance extremely simple and rude'.[2]

T.H. Green (1836–1882), the British Liberalist philosopher stated that 'the empires in the East are, in the main, tax-collecting institutions. They exercise coercive power on their subjects of the most violent kind (and) do not impose laws as distinct from particular and occasional commands.'[3] It is noticeable that as a philosopher Green is famous for his 'concept of moral freedom' and emphasis on the rights of the people. In this socio-democratic perspective, he assessed the Asian state-system and upheld the notion of oriental despotism.

Even the Romantic historians like Mountstuart Elphinstone, who was very sensitive to the uniqueness of India's past, remarks that 'the government in ancient India was vested in an absolute Monarch and he (the king) was subject indeed to no legal control by human authority'.[4] He admits that the ruler was, according to *Dharmasastras*, bound to follow certain rules and there was provision for censure as well, but adds that 'No means are provided for enforcing those penalties and neither the councils nor the military chiefs appear to have possessed any constitutional power but what they derived from his (ruler's) will.[5]

With the beginning of the 20th century, imperialist historiography reflected some modifications which may be attributed to nationalist resurgence and the change in methodology of history-writing itself. T.W. Rhys Davids approached the state-system of ancient India in a seemingly unorthodox manner in his work *Buddhist India* (1903). Apart from Brahamanical law books, he studied Buddhist sources and made a departure point by pronouncing the existence of the republic kingdoms, besides the monarchy in ancient India. In Rhys Davids' opinion, 'Brahimin books convey the impression that the only recognised, and in fact universally prevalent, form of government was that of kings under the guidance and tutelage of priests.'[6]

Exclusive dependence on Brahminical sources for the study of state not only led republics to go unnoticed but also created the impression of undue priestly element in the polity. In brief, most imperialist historians interpreted the state in ancient India as despotic, theocratic, and exploitative institution. They also professed that 'rule of law' and 'welfare of the people' were concepts alien to the political theorists of ancient India. It is these assumptions which invited sharp reactions from the nationalist historians in the latter half of the 19th century and afterwards.

Nationalist View of the Nature of State

In the nationalist perception state in ancient India was a 'benevolent institute which not only protected the life of the people but also strived for the general welfare'. D.R. Bhandarkar reflects the crux of the nationalist vision when he observes 'Protection of life and property and the administration of justice were not the only functions of the Hindu state. It had also to take cognizance of a number of philanthropic, intellectual and above all economic necessities'.[7]

It is noticeable that any discussion about the nature and concept of state is often entangled with the notion of kingship in ancient India. The most dominant form of the state in ancient India was monarchy. Traces of republicanism can be found in many tribal oligarchies, but they were not frequent in their historical emergence. Bhandarkar in this regards observes 'the king, being the soul of the body politic, thus represents the state.'[8] Similar view is reflected in the works of P.N. Banerji, Beni Prasad, P.V. Kane, among others. Beni Prasad supposes that 'lack of permanent natural boundaries among the states in north India and philosophy of universal dominion as an ideal before the king, resulted in incessant warfare or readiness for war. It would promote monarchy as against any other form of government'.[9] P.V. Kane holds the view that in ancient India the word *Rajya* is used for: kingdom (mostly), state and government.[10]

Nationalist scholars observed that definition of state as reflected in *Saptanga* theory of Kautilya is very much similar to those given in modern times. Territory, population, government, sovereignty, which according to modern political thinkers constitute a 'state' are proved to be present in the ancient Indian concept of state. Bhandarakar says, '*Janapada* denotes both population and territory which form the physical constituents of the state from the stand-point of modern political science.'[11] Unity and governmental organisation which fall under sovereignty, is reflected through *swami*, *amatya*. *Swamin* which means the 'lord or sovereign', shows that the territory of which he is the lord must denote an independent entity, not forming part of a wider political unit.'[12] The distinction between governors and governed is also present. *Swamin* and *amatyas* are invested with the authority to govern and the *Janapada* forming the population denotes the individuals who render obedience.[13] *Durga*, *kosa*, and *danda* were different means through which state can enforce its will.[14]

Most of the nationalist historians went to the extent of tracing many modern days' concepts like 'organic notion of state' democracy, trusteeship, welfare state, socialism and decentralization. Their purpose was to challenge imperialist idea of European monopoly over these concepts. The organic theory of state, propagated mainly by idealist and totalitarian philosophers asserts that state is a body and its different parts consisting of individuals perform special functions assigned to them. Such a concept has been proved by nationalist historian to be present in the writings of ancient political thinkers of India as well. Bhandarkar opines that 'state is looked upon by the authors of the Hindu polity also as a living spiritual organism, where the swamin was the soul and the other six *prakritis* or natural constituents, the body of the state'.[15]

Nationalist historians, led by K.P. Jayaswal, propounded the notion that the state in ancient India was concerned with the well-being of the masses and always cherished the values and ideals of democracy. Jayaswal quite candidly underlines the fact that 'state under Monarchy in the eyes of the Hindus was a trust'.[16] The trust, the state thus created for the prosperity of the people. It is this underlying principle which ...

culminated in the fixed maxim that the king is the servant of the people getting his wages.'[17] Dikshitar talks of the existence of common will as the base of any legal system and asserts that this common will is nothing but the expression of healthy public opinion which is a feature of ancient Indian democracy'.[18]

Socialism is also said to be present in the nature of state in ancient India. Bhandarkar thinks that the general policies followed by the Kautilyan state were akin to modern concept of socialism. He observes, 'those who have read *Kautilya* carefully cannot fail to be impressed by the state policy which is fairly well indicated in his work and which looks like modern state socialism'.[19] In support of his hypothesis, he has highlighted the Kautilyan policy of state control over all the natural and human resources by many *Adhyakshas* or superintendents.

It is matter of fact that a socialist state system often implies the greater amount of control over every walk of life; but nationalist historians simultaneously stress on the existence of individual liberty and decentralization in ancient India. Altekar says, 'The principle of decentralization was carried to a very great extent and extensive powers were delegated to the village panchayats, city councils and trade guilds, and the state carried on its socialistic activities with the active cooperation of these popular bodies. There was hardly any encroachment on the individual liberty'.[20] He adds, 'ancient Indians permitted the state a wider sphere of activity not because they did not value individual liberty but because they felt that the state could organise them by reconciling conflicting interests'.[21]

U.N. Ghoshal speaks of welfare state in ancient India with its programme of universal protection and state relief to the poor and needy.[22] Kane by analysing *Dharmasastras* takes the four *purusharthas – dharma, artha, kama, moksha* – to be the guiding principles of state policy in ancient India.[23] Nationalist historians also exonerate the state from being responsible for social inequality and thus hindering egalitarianism. Bhandarkar remarks that the state in ancient India was not interested in enforcing caste iniquities. If any case actually arose, they must have been decided by the caste or the village panchayats, which were purely non official bodies.[24] He further says that the iniquities of Hindu social order was due to narrow-mindedness of Hindu society of the age and not to the states making *dharma* as one of its aims.[25] But scholars like Beni Prasad do not agree to this assumption, though they acknowledge many humanitarian features of the state in ancient India. Beni Prasad comments, 'it (state) fell a victim to caste and deliberately refused to bring the lower classes into line with the rest of Hindu society or to encourage their higher life. It allied itself with priest craft and conservatism and helped perpetuate the distinction between man and man'.[26] This difference of opinion displays different sub-streams within the flow of nationalist historiography of the state in ancient India.

Religious or priestly element in ancient Indian legal institutions is likely to leave an impression of theocratic state. But P.N. Banerjee among others asserts, 'although the social organization contained within its bosom the Brahmanic theocracy and was to a large extent dominated by it, the state itself never became a theocracy in the proper sense of the term'.[27] The reasons given by him are: first, the ruler was never regarded as the head of religion. Secondly, the primary object of the state was not spiritual salvation but social well being. Thirdly, political status of individuals was independent of their religious beliefs and convictions.[28]

Nationalist View of the Origin of the State

While conceptualising the origin of state, we come across many modern theories, among which mainly the twin tradition of 'divine origin' and 'contract theory' are projected in ancient Indian perspective. Theory of divine origin supposes that to overcome a situation of anarchy and chaos, God created the institution of kingship whose basic function is to maintain law and order. Most nationalist historians assume that ancient Indian literature on polity and law is galore in depicting the theory of divine origin in one or another form.

D.R. Bhandarkar feels that the theory of divine origin in nascent state can be traced in *Yajus-Samhitas* and *Brahamanas*, especially *Taitriya* and *Satapatha*; but its fullest expression is found in the views of *Manu* and *Bhism* where the king is not just the abode of regent gods like *Yama, Kubera, Vayu*, etc., but created by the supreme God *Prajapati*. Quoting the verse from *Manu* where it is mentioned that king is not only a deity but also a creation of the Supreme, Bhandarkar says, 'for the first time therefore we find a trace of the real divine origin of the kingship similar to that propounded by western thinkers.'[29] U.N. Ghoshal traces the genesis of the theory of divine origin to the Vedic dogma of creation of the four castes – involving the notion that *Kshatriyas* or the ruling order was invested with political authority by divine ordination.[30]

Most nationalist scholars believe that theory of social contract dates earlier to the notion of Divine Origin. The contract theory, as conceived by western philosophers (Hobbes, Locke, Rousseau) presupposes three essential factors: (i) the state of nature; (ii) the social compact; and (iii) governmental compact. It asserts that the state is an outcome of contract between the ruler and the ruled and it was in return for the services the king rendered to the people that he received their obedience and their contributions for the maintenance of royalty.

K.P. Jayaswal claims that political writers of ancient India held that the king was elected on certain grounds or a contract, and that original contract was always enforced subsequently ... this contract found support in Vedic hymns and songs of royal election, in rituals of royal consecration which were based on elective principles, and in the coronation oath which made the king swear that he should rule according to law.[31] But in U.N. Ghoshal's opinion it was not Brahmanic but Buddhist accounts that clearly demonstrate social contract theory. He asserts, 'Neither the Brahmanic nor the Jain theories involve the conception of the creation of the society or the state or both by contract.'[32] Ghoshal held that 'The Buddhist theory furnishes a quasi-historical justification for the principle of contract by tracing the creation of the state to a bilateral governmental compact made by the people with their original ruler for escaping the evils of the state of nature'.[33]

Ghoshal has aptly compared the ancient Indian version of social contract with its European counterpart in the 'general summary' and 'conclusion' of his book. For example, he says, in the West, the authority and sovereignty of the ruler were derived from the community, which in turn led to the doctrine of resistance of the subjects against the ruler. Whereas in Indian theory, the reciprocal rights and duties of the king and his subjects are founded on law (*Dharma*); but this is derived from the joint source of canon and custom, and not from a mutual agreement (between king and community) forming the basis of those relations.[34]

Most nationalist historians regard contract theory as more dominant notion to explain the origin of state in ancient India, in comparison to the theory of divine origin. This historiographical propensity among nationalists can be attributed to many factors. The contract theory owing to its historical nature leaves little space for religion in the origin of the state and thus reflects a secular aspect of the polity and law. So this could help nationalists in countering the imperialist notion which took the impact of religion to be all pervasive. Besides, the idea of social contract is often in vicinity with the mechanistic theory of the state, and thereby confirms the basic tenets of liberalism and individualism. This again could nullify the imperialist notion of 'Oriental Despotism', characterized by the absence of individual rights.

Marxist View of State in Ancient India

The Marxist analysis of the nature and origin of state in ancient India is in the light of dialectics and historical materialism. Marx himself has not given any detailed description of the origin of state; he was concerned more with the nature of the state. It is his friend Fredrick Engels' *The Origin of the Family, Private Property and the State* (1884) that the state is taken to be the necessary consequence of the class-division, which has influenced Marxist interpretation of the emergence of state in ancient India.

Ram Sharan Sharma and Romila Thapar are the leading Marxist historians who studied the rise and growth of the state. They perceive the origin of state as a process of formation, not as a sudden event as is assumed in the theories of social contract and divine origin. Both underline the importance of material factors reflected well in the changing pattern and technique of agriculture among others. R.S. Sharma presents a historical survey of state formation in various stages of ancient Indian polity. He writes, 'given their material life and tribal structure, the Rig Vedic people were not capable of developing any advanced political system which can be called state either in the ancient Indian or the modern sense of the term .... Although the term *rajan* is used for the Rig Vedic chiefs, the nature of the Rig Vedic kingship was basically the same as chiefship'.[35] He opines that the later Vedic polity assumed the character of 'proto-state' with royal power and administrative structure, but could not witness the emergence of full-fledged state because the surplus available from agriculture was still marginal.[36]

According to Prof. Sharma, the origin and growth of taxation system determines the rise and development of the state.[37] The sound taxation presupposes surplus production in agriculture which was made possible in Buddhist period owing to widespread use of iron technology. Besides, 'coercion' had to be applied to get the surplus and it was strengthened by the installation of collectors backed by professional soldiers and priestly propaganda.[38] All these favourable conditions facilitated the 'state formation in northern India' in the pre-Mauryan times and onwards. This is what R.S. Sharma tried to establish in his *Aspects of Political Ideas and Institutions in Ancient India.*

Romila Thapar attributes the rise of state to the transformation of 'lineage society' (or tribal society) into a class divided society. For her, stratification is a precondition to the emergence of the state since stratified groups become involved in internal conflicts, require contracts for agreements or result in the evolution of a powerful elite.[39] She writes,

> 'In the middle Ganga valley rice agriculture and irrigation were initially important but probably were not sufficient causes. However, they sharpened stratification between those who owned the land and those who laboured on it. The imminence of internal tension made the possibility of control through a state system feasible. The recognizable state emerges when the stratification is much more widespread both socially and geographically.'[40]

Like the origin, nature of the state in ancient India has too been examined by Marxist historians. R.S. Sharma has challenged different explanations – such as ecological, geographical, sociological, ownership of the land and self-sufficiency of villages – given for the justification of western notion of 'oriental despotism'. For example, regarding the theory that large-scale irrigation, requiring central authority caused Asiatic despot (hydraulic despotism), he says, 'Only the north-western part of the Indian subcontinent is arid, otherwise its major part has plenty of rain ... embankment of *Sudarshan* lake ... shows that irrigation was a provincial responsibility. Evidence of family and communal construction of irrigation works is not lacking'.[41] Finally, Prof. Sharma comments that the theory of oriental despotism by western scholars was meant to serve as a garb for colonial aggression.[42]

R.S. Sharma believes that state is defined for the first time in the *Arthsastra* of Kautilya as consisting of seven elements (*saptanga*), and it happened only after the rise of the well-organised states of *Kosala* and *Magadha* in the age of Buddha.[43] This interpretation is consistent with the Marxist notion in which 'form' or 'idea' is supposed to follow 'matter'. Sharma has explained the seven elements – *swami, amatya, janapada, durga, kosa, danda* and *mitra* – found in *Arthasastra* and other Brahmanical texts, and compared them with the modern constituents of the state. He observes that four essential elements of the modern state: sovereignty, government, territory and population are covered respectively by *svami, amatya,* and *janapada* in the *saptanga* theory.[44] Commenting on the near absence of army (*dand*), taxation *(kosa)*, capital (*durga)* and ally (*mitra)* in the modern definition of state, he says, 'it sounds to be abstract in contrast to the ancient definition, which was concrete and eminently practical'.[45]

R.S. Sharma compares the practical nature of Kautilyan state with that of the state set forth by Engels, who emphasises the class character of the state. He identifies the public officials, public power, and taxes mentioned by Engels with the *amatyas, danda* and *kosa* of *Arthsastra* respectively. This similarity, says Sharma, is 'because both the schools (Kautilyan and Marxist) stress that the theory should reflect practice. They come to grips with the realities of political life and are not lost in the claptrap of empty forms'.[46]

The Post-colonial Perception of State in Ancient India

After India's freedom in 1947 and beginning of the process of decolonization globally, state in ancient India came to be viewed with new approaches and dimensions. Scholars like J. Gonda and Charles Drekmeier try to explain the process of state formation through the methods of cultural anthropology and sociology. For them, the ritualistic and religious devices were so designed that they resulted in the concentration of power into the hands of upper classes. Charles Drekmeier writes in the preface of his book *Kingship and Community in Early India* (1962) that 'the impression of a mindless, jewel-bedecked despotism colours the picture of the ancient East in many Western mind. This book is intended to correct that image.'[47] He observes that 'in Hindu political philosophy, unlike Western tradition the theory of divine origin is distinct with that of divine right. Never was the Hindu king vested with the divine right. The *Mahabharata*, the *smritis*, the *puranas*, and the other texts refer to a functional similarity of the kings to the gods'.[48] He adds,

> 'The concept of the king's quasi-divinity was never intended to justify irresponsible rule; it served as a means of promoting deference to authority. The counsel of *Bhisma* is as a representative of Hindu theory. The saga observes that the king who fails to protect his subjects must be slain like a mad dog. This is sufficient to suggest that the king did not rule by divine right as defined by the Stuart kings.'[49]

Some European Indologists and legal historians of the post-colonial period have studied the state system in ancient India with a comparatively more balanced and sensitive approach. Robert Lingat, too, opposes the alleged autocratic nature of the kingship. He says 'the authority of the king is balanced by the privileged situation of the Brahmins. If the king were to disdain the advice of his Brahmins, he would not only fail in his duty, but even incur the risk of governing badly'.[50] However Lingat does not view this relation between two powers for analogy with the Christian theory of the 'Two Swords'. He remarks, 'There are no two powers here each functioning in its proper sphere, the sacred to each other, and the profane to the other. Secular power alone has the capacity to act, but it is blind force which needs to be directed before its application can be effectual.'[51]

Regarding the divinity of the king, Lingat appears close to the views of Drekmeier, when he remarks, 'it is only by exercising the royal function as it was created by the gods that the king is assimilated to a deity. The dominant idea of the *Dharamsastra* writers seems to have been that it was not the king who had a divine nature, but the royal function itself'.[52]

J.D.M. Derrett analyses the practical and theoretical standpoints related to the rise of state which he prefers to call 'empire'. Regarding the practical aspect Derrett says,

> 'At the edges of cultivation and civilization protection of the settlements was a full-time task for someone: and nearly always beyond the means of cultivators themselves. Hence, the need for subjection to an imperial power which could levy taxes for protection over a wide area, thus spreading the burden, and with the proceeds employ standing forces to police the frontiers.'[53]

Derrett then comments that empire would be extended not merely by conquest but also by belief that the imperial family intended to facilitate or foster a particular ideological approach to life, private and public, hence the ideological factor must not be ignored.[54] In his opinion 'the Mauryan connection with Buddhism, and the attitude of later emperors to religious questions, cannot be shown not to have had a role to play in the willingness of people to subject themselves to this rule, or to remain subject to it against fissiparous tendencies'.[55]

From the above survey, it is obvious that different historians have given different interpretations of the origin and nature of sate in ancient India. The imperialist and western writers were driven by the notion of 'oriental despotism' and nourished the view that religion and rituals played essential role in the emergence of state in early India. In the nationalist writings, the earliest state of India came to be viewed as the result of a contract between the ruler and the ruled. It was imagined that the state in ancient India was democratic and limited which on its part could not have been; but the result of the initial contract. The Marxist historians tried to explain the formation and nature of the state in the light of socio-economic processes.

It is difficult to decide that which of the interpretations is pertinent. However, it can be argued that the formation of the state in ancient India was a long-drawn process combining all the factors of historical change, be it geographical, ideological, technological or socio-economic. So any approach to understand the origin of state must be holistic and evolutionary in its theoretical model. Similar is the need for the study of the nature of state also. This tendency to some extent is seen in some post-colonial studies on the growth and nature of state in ancient India.

State as a Source of Law

In the second chapter entitled 'The Concept of Hindu Law' it has been made clear that most historians take *Sruti, Smriti* and custom to be the chief sources of Hindu law. In their perception, state or/and the king were not the makers of the law, instead executive bodies to carry out the dharma (law), based on canon and custom. But many other historians talk of king's legislative power and thereby delineate the state in ancient India as a source of law also. It is to be noted that law made by kings is reflected in the form of 'royal edicts' and is entirely different from canon or'sacred law'. It was a kind of administrative law, distinct from basic constitutional law in the modern sense and therefore has been termed by some historians as 'state law'.

Western historians viewed the state in ancient India with the prism of 'Oriental Despotism' which implies that the king monopolized all the legislative powers along with executive and judicial ones. James Mill commented, 'In the first place, there are hardly any laws, the king alone is entitled to judge, who is entitled to legislate, since he must make law for every occasion'.[56]

But since the notion of the 'Oriental Despotism' itself has been rejected, the idea of centralization of legislative rights in king cannot be held anymore. Similarly, extremist is the theory which entirely overlooks the law-making capacity of the kings in favour of the predominance of Dharmsastric laws in ancient India. For the instance, K.P. Jayaswal observed that there was the all-powerful law, the common law of the Hindus, which is declared again and again to be above the king and as the king of the kings.[57] He adds: 'Even in the palmiest days of Hindu Monarchy, neither in the *Manava-Dharma-Sastra* nor in the *Arhta-Sastra*, was the king placed above the law. He could make new laws according to the *Artha-Sastra*, according to Manu he could not; but when he could make laws he passed only regulatory laws and not laws substantive or laws making him arbitrary'.[58]

However, those historians who focus on *Arthasastra* school of thoughts and on text like *Narad Smriti*, acknowledge the king's power to frame laws. U.N. Ghoshal believes that in *Kautilya*'s thought, there emerged a new conception, namely that of the king's quasi-legislative authority.[59] Ghoshal writes,

> 'Kautilya classifies the king's writs (*sasana*) under eight heads with appropriate titles ... Mention may also be made of the elaborate regulations evidently issued under the king's authority for the guidance of the administrative heads (*adhyakshas*), as well as the panels of magistrates in the charge of administrative courts. It follows from the above that the king's executive edict is invested in *Kautilya*'s thought with the force of law.'[60]

Ghoshal also points out the four feet of the subject matter of a lawsuit in modes of decision in *Arthsastra*. These are *dharma, vyavahara, charitra* and *rajsasana*. In his opinion, the *rajsasna* which is identical with the king's decree is said to prevail over the first three processes.[61] In this regards he writes, 'In the history of our juristic and political ideas this reference to the overriding authority of the king's decree over all other judicial processes is of high significance, for it clearly and unequivocally enumerates for the first time the principle of the king's judicial sovereignty.'[62]

Robert Lingat has analysed the king's legislative power in a greater detail. Firstly, he clarifies that 'legislative power' is a right attributed to a constitutionally competent authority to pronounce rules having a general application and processing in principle, a permanent character. Particular orders, for example, would not be legislation within this definition.[63] With this parameter, Lingat rejects Derrett's view that the king's intervention for agreements between local groups is an indirect form of legislative activity.[64]

Lingat does not see legislative element in the royal sanction and approval to compacts, conventions or regulations. He writes, 'When the king confirms any such regulations, he apparently acts not as a legislator but as an administrator concerned to keep the peace between his subjects.'[65] He adds that far from legislating in the sphere reserved for *srotriyas*, the kings of the history tried to enlighten their subjects and themselves upon their duties, giving their patronage to commentators and digest-writers. This was the only way in which they acquired renown as pious princes, devoted to dharma.[66]

However, Lingat admits that the legislative activity of the king was limited very seriously, but there did remain a vast field in which it might operate. He says, 'The majority of the topics which come within what we would call administrative law fell under royal authority. The *dharma-sastras* confine themselves to indicating, for example, the qualities which ministers should have. But it fell to the king to divide amongst them the task of administration, to define the scope and the powers of each ministry.'[67] He further writes, 'It seems impossible that every section of the administrative machine could have functioned under the direct orders of the king. The continuity of the institutions must have demanded royal instructions having the effect of the laws.'[68]

Now it can safely be concluded that not only Kautilyan polity, but in every state system, the king seemed to enjoy right to regulate their internal administration. King's decrees, which were sometimes manifested in epigraphic forms, drew same respect and obedience as any of sacred canon. They belong to positive law, law-in-action, immediately applicable to the subjects. This doubtlessly positions state as a source of law also.

Revenue Regulations

The mode of taxation – or broadly speaking revenue system – is often the indicative of the nature of state itself. Whether the state is a welfare entity or an autocratic one can well be understood through its taxation policy. Therefore, while studying ancient Indian laws and polity, Europeans took keen interest in viewing the contemporary taxes. But their interpretations went almost in accordance with general imperialist assumption of India, and so were challenged by nationalist historians. Marxists' belief in 'economic determinism' automatically led them to in-depth analysis of ancient Indian taxation. Consequently, several models of interpreting the revenue regulations in ancient India emerged. This very interesting aspect of historical studies can well be discussed in the order of historiographical development in India.

James Mill, perhaps the first most comprehensive modern historian of ancient India, is of the opinion that it is nothing but taxation that affects the state of people to a greater extent. He observes that in Hindu Laws, an enumeration of all the objects of taxation is found. There exists the taxes on the produce of land and labour, tax on accumulation, on sales and pole tax.[69] Commenting on the first type of tax, i.e., tax on the produce of soil, he says that it offends against the *rule of certainty* to high degree as it varies from sixth to twelfth part of the total produce.[70] Mill asserts 'This uncertainty opens a boundless field to all the wretched arts of the chicanery and fraud on the part of people, and all the evils of oppression on the part of the collectors'.[71] He continues that whenever an option is granted between less taxation and greater, the violent propensity of all imperfect governments to excess in expense is sure in time to establish the greater. This is why, concludes Mill, that a sixth part of the produce became the uniform tax in Hindustan.[72]

Mill's perception was further strengthened by his followers of imperialist mind. They assumed that the state in India was primarily a tax-collecting institution and the incidence of taxation was oppressive. Such stereotypes weres criticized by the Indian nationalist historians. K.P. Jayaswal says that the canons of taxation settled by constitutional writers agree with the aims for which the Hindu state was created, namely, 'for prosperity, land-culture, wealth and well-being'.[73] He further adds 'The principles, guiding the taxation policy, were not dependent on the whims and fancies of king but on law. Taxes had been fixed by law and the scales had been embodied in the sacred common law, the consequence was that whatever be the form of government, the matter of taxation was not an object of the ruler's caprice'.[74] The economic ground on which the tax system was based was sound and reasonable. Ability and least sacrifice were the guiding principles of the framers of the financial regulations of ancient India.[75]

U.N. Ghoshal published his specific book on taxation, entitled *Contributions to the History of the Hindu Revenue System* in 1929. Reflecting a nationalist zeal, he stated that the 'principles of early Indian taxation surpass the achievements of classical antiquity and tend to approach the ideas of European thinkers in the 18th and early 19th centuries'.[76] In his opinion, the view that the taxes are the king's dues for the service of protection is identical with the similar doctrine of 17th and 18th century Europe.[77]

A.S. Altekar, representing the nationalist views and notions at large, has summarized the principles of taxation propounded by the *Smritis* and epics as following:

1. The taxation was to be reasonable and equitable; which meant that the state on the one side and the agriculturist or the traders on the other both should feel that they have got a fair and reasonable return for their labours.
2. In the case of trade and industry, the taxation was to be on net profits and not on gross earnings.
3. An article was to be taxed only once and not twice.
4. Extra taxation was to be imposed only in the times of national calamity after taking comprehensive steps to explain the situation to the people with a view to ensure a willing response.[78]

Similar kinds of principles of taxation were earlier pronounced by K.P. Jayaswal, when he said,

> 'Economic considerations are everywhere prominent. Productive power is not to be hampered; profit and not capital is to be taxed; articles which lead to new industries are to be encouraged; exports which cause 'artificial' prosperity by driving up prices are to be discouraged; no special protection is granted to ordinary industries; taxes should be gradual, and with reference to capacity, and not in an obnoxious form.'[79]

Altekar says that *Smritis* lay down no uniform rate of taxation (a tendency which James Mill earlier has criticized as a cause of uncertainty); but the normal procedure, however, was to charge one sixth of the produce as land tax.[80] When the cultivator suffered losses, the state used to remit or reduce the taxes as demanded by situation.[81] There being no permanent settlement of the land tax (like *Zamidari* system of British India) and *Smritis* permitting large variation in percentage, taxes could be enhanced when required by the exigencies of the state finance.[82]

R.S. Sharma has emphasized on the importance of tax system in ancient India. He claims that the origin and growth of the taxation system determines the rise and development of the state.[83] Instead of giving any sweeping generalization for whole ancient India, Prof. Sharma speaks of changing pattern of taxation. He observes that the list of taxes enumerated in the *Arthasastra* of *Kautilya* is much larger than that found in Gupta inscriptions, which would suggest that the burden of taxation decreased in Gupta times.[84] Of the emergency taxes recommended in *Arthasastra,* there is no trace in Gupta times.[85] In fact the principles of taxation which enjoin the king to leave enough subsistence to the producer were the products of the early centuries of the Christian era and may have influenced the fiscal policy of the rulers of this period.[86] This change has been attributed to the shrinkage in the size of Gupta bureaucracy. Since the Guptas, says Prof. Sharma, did not maintain a large administrative establishment, so they did not require as many taxes as the Mauryas did.[87]

A high degree of debate exists among historians regarding the proprietorship in land. This is important from the point of taxation policy. If the ownership of the land is vested with the king, then the amount paid by cultivator would be land rent not land tax. James Mill has opined that property of soil resided in the sovereign; for if it did not reside in him, it will be impossible to show to whom it belonged.[88] He says that every European visitor before East India Company's implementation of permanent settlement in Bengal (1793) has agreed to the notion of royal ownership of land.[89] Same idea is echoed in the observation by Vincent Smith. Based on certain instances from law books like that of Manu, accounts of foreign travellers and land grants, he held the view that 'the native law of India had always recognized agricultural land as being crown property.'[90] Such a view point was vehemently criticized by latter nationalist historians.

K.P. Jayaswal, rejecting the notion, comments:

> 'The writers (European) unconsciously have read his own feudal law into Hindu Jurisprudence. Nothing is as distant from Hindu Law as this theory. Numerous instances of gifts and sales of land by private individuals can be given from the earliest literature. Law books give provisions for sale of land and acquirement of property right by prescription. Inscriptions proving to the hilt private property in the soil are extant. Above all, it is expressly and emphatically declared that the king has no property in the soil and this is declared in no less authority than the very logic of Hindu law, the Mimansa.'[91]

A.S. Altekar too upholds the findings of Jayaswal. He observes; 'in the post-Buddhist period at any rate the ownership in cultivable land was vested in private individuals; the state could not interfere with it except for the non-payment of the land tax. What is claimed from the average cultivator was thus not a land rent but a land tax.[92] He argued that some state grants recorded the gifts of entire villages to Brahamanas or temples, but this does not support the theory of state ownership of the arable land. For what the grants assign in most of these cases is the state's right to receive various taxes, including land tax. They never effect any change in the private ownership of the landed property included in the village.[93]

Karl Marx, himself dwelling on the subject, initially accepted Bernier's theory regarding royal proprietorship of all land in India. Later, he is said to have recognized three forms of land tenure in India – communal property, private property and feudal property; of these the first two relate to ancient India, however in early medieval times there is strong evidence for royal ownership of land as well as some kind of feudal property in land.[94]

R.S. Sharma believes that evidence for royal ownership of land in ancient times including the all powerful *Kautilayan* state is weak. However, the situation began to change in the second century AD, and over a considerable part of the country in the Gupta period. But it was in early medieval period when process of kings' ownership over the land rights becomes common.[95] This view is supported by the facts that the early medieval law books emphasize royal lordship over the land and king claimed for *bhoga* which earlier was a voluntary periodical supply of fuel, fruits and flowers. But in addition to royal rights in land, there developed in early medieval period feudal property in land, limiting the kings' dominion over the soil. This trend resulted in the transfer of royal right to the enjoyment of all agrarian resources to the intermediate landlords.[96]

Besides the land tax, trade and industry formed significant source of revenue. Being indirect taxes, they were the key-note of taxation policy. 'Hindu politicians disliked direct taxation. They had practically no direct tax in their system except the produce tax. Import duties which were exclusively 'indirect' in their incidence were the next great tax after the product tax.'[97]

Vishti or forced unpaid labour, which is often criticized as oppressive, is taken by many nationalist historians to represent a form of tax. K.P. Jayaswal observes, 'Poor people could afford to pay a tax neither in cash nor in kind, but it was felt that they also should pay something to state in return for the protection they got from it. This they could do most conveniently by offering free service to the state.'[98] Moreover, it was not the state, but the local bodies (barring a few cases) which had the right to extract this labour in order to carry out their public works programmes.[99]

It has been often highlighted that the principles of taxation, as laid down in *Smritis* and other sources are 'ideals' which were not followed in real life. Moreover, there are references in literature and inscriptions also to show that taxation was often oppressive. Scholars like Altekar do not subscribe to such views. He is of the opinion that instances of oppression were rare and the Kashmiri tyrants often referred to were exceptions. Evidence is available to show that people could successfully oppose the levy of unjust taxes imposed by the state.[100] Village assemblies and their executives were usually strong enough to resist encroachments on their legitimate rights and interests.[101]

An assessment of the above-discussed models to understand the ancient Indian revenue regulations may easily indicate that they almost are based on certain pre-conceived notions. Variation in land tax rates has been viewed by James Mill as a *rule* of *uncertainty*; but it was due to the difference in productivity of many kinds of land. The change in tax rate in accordance with the fertility of land has always been a sound economic idea. As regards the proprietorship of land, it is more logical to see that as an ever-changing concept, as has been studied by R.S. Sharma. The oppressive nature of ancient Indian taxation is not supported much by sufficient evidences. Though we cannot rule out exploitative aspect of *vishti* like taxes in early medieval times; but it was not a general trend pervading all phases of ancient India. Contrary to this, ancient India did witness some benevolent kings like Ashoka (273–236 BC), and much later Chola Kulottung I (1070–1120 AD) who lessened the tax burden. So the study of revenue regulations in ancient India has to be more fact-based, holistic and coherent with contemporary historical perspective.

International Laws

International laws are the rules of conduct which form the basis of international relations. Their basic purpose is to prevent wars and promote peace amongst nations. In ancient India – unlike modern nations – there were smaller independent states which sometimes rose to the status of big empires. The political ideal of *Chackravartin* (universal dominion) and absence of natural boundaries, particularly in North India, seems to have tempted the estates to encroach upon the territories of each other. The resultant instability and uncertainty necessitated the formulation of certain principles to conduct the inter-state relations.

Western critique imbued with imperialistic proclivity denied that ancient Indians had any knowledge of international law. How could a race, which knew nothing about the nation, chart out rules of international conduct was one of the typical Western outlooks. Scholars like Hall considered international law as a 'favoured monopoly' of the European family of nations.[102] But nationalist historians not only projected the existence of the 'nation-states' in early India; but also claimed that Indians had knowledge of international law according to which they carried their international conduct.

S.V. Viswanatha maintains that rules guiding the international relations were derived from dharma, the basic tenets of which prevailed all over India. Even though, there was no single authority who 'formulated' and 'enforced' the idea of dharma, the fear of Almighty resulted in total subservience of people to it. Thus, in India, the general rules of international conduct were already in existence and the nations had only to act up to them unquestionably.[103] He observes that the accepted division of modern international law are war, peace and neutrality. In India also it may be said that these divisions held good in general.[104]

The twin principles which are said to have guided the international law were self-preservation and balance of power among different states. In this regard, Viswanath remarks:

> 'A *mandala* consisted of twelve kings in which ambitious conqueror was situated at the centre. He was surrounded by a host of the kings friendly, hostile and neutral. The king at the centre was to develop such a relation with these states, so that he not only succeeds in self preservation, but also manages to enhance his power. If the king is attacked, the intervening states were likely to form coalitions to resist the invasion so that the balance of power is not tampered with.'[105]

A.S. Altekar, too, follows the same line and comments, '*Smriti* writers and political thinkers in ancient India knew that war could not be altogether tabooed. A judicious balance of power among different states was advocated and elaborate rules of warfare aimed at minimising the loss to person and property were laid down. The well-known *mandala* theory of the *Smriti* and *Niti* writers is based upon this principle.'[106] He further says that the theory that immediate neighbouring states are inimical seems to be natural. The enmity between France and Germany, between Poland and Russia, between China and Japan, was largely due to their contiguity which often caused conflicts of interests.[107]

The nationalist historians explained that the 'concept of war' was also conceived by the ancient Indian thinkers. Viswanatha views the wars in ancient India as the last option, used only when the conduct of belligerent states necessitated breaking off negotiations.[108] Wholesale devastation and ruthless destruction was not resorted to. Tillers of the soil and those people who were engaged in special arts were to be exempted. As in modern international codes, works of religion and fine arts and the persons that were employed in dressing the wounded and the sick or were engaged in scientific pursuits were not to be subjected to the risks of war, but special protection was given to them.[109]

Altekar describes the concept of *dharmayudha* in ancient India and remarks that defeated territory was not annexed in general. If, however, annexation became inevitable, established laws and customs were respected and the life and property of the new subjects were protected. Internal autonomy was easily conceded.[110]

P.N. Banerjee states that in ancient India alliances were made by means of treatises.[111] The observance of a treaty either depended upon the plighted word (*satya, sapatha*) or was enforced by means of sureties (*pratibhu*) and hostages (*pratigraha*), when there was an apprehension of breach of faith.[112]

In the opinion of nationalist historians, diplomacy in the form of regular exchanges of foreign envoys between states has been a very important part of international conduct in ancient India. Banerjee translates various types of diplomats, *Nisristartha, Duta, Parimitartha* and *Sasanahara* as l messagesPlenipotentiaries, Ambassadors, charge d'affaires and conveyors of royal messages, respectively. However, in general language the term *Dutah* was used to cover all these forms.[113] The sacredness and inviolability of the person of ambassadors was respected. As the representative of a foreign power, an envoy enjoyed great privileges and immunities.[114]

In addition to diplomats, there were 'spies' and other 'news agents' who formed in themselves as a sort of international agents.[115] Reacting to Smith's remarks that use of espionage for international dealings implied 'inveterate and universal suspicion', Viswanatha points out that 'such has been the case in all ages among all nations as regards dealings in international politics.'[116]

Viswanatha among others holds the view that besides the sovereign and independent states, part sovereign and feudatory or semi-independent states existed in large numbers in ancient India. These kinds of states were also subjected to the international law in ancient India.[117]

R.S. Sharma doubted the application of *mandala* theory to the time of Kautilya and held that it is not typical of Maurya time. He claims that 'it would be ridiculous to apply the *Mandala* theory or the idea of circle of kings enumerated by Kautilya to the Maurya empire'.[118] He further observes that 'really *Mandala* theory reflects some sort of feudal relationship and seems to have been inserted in the *Arthshastr*a in early medieval times. Significantlly enough the term Mandala is not known to ancient inscriptions'.[119] The likelihood of insertion of some portions in *Arthashastra* cannot be denied but most historians of different schools attribute the *Mandala* theory to Kautilya's *Arthashastra*.

In light of above studies, it can undisputedly be summarized that ancient India witnessed much progress in framing the rules to guide the relation between two states. *Mandala* theory, six-fold policy (*shadgunya niti* – 1. *Sandhi,* 2. *Vigrah,* 3. *Asana,* 4. *Yana,* 5. *Sansraya, and* 6. *Dvaidhibhava*) and four measures (*sama, dama, danda* and *bheda)* as delineated in *Arthashastra* were extremely pragmatic, shrewd, excellent, and they remained almost unsurpassed in the ancient world. Respect for inter-state rules in ancient India becomes more significant when we look at the fact that in the West obvious acceptance of international law between two states began only with the treaty of Westphalia in 1648. Though it is too enthusiastic to trace all facets of modern international law in ancient India; but no legal historian can overlook the early Indian achievements in this field.

Notes

1. Mill, James, *The History of British India*, Vol. II, p. 175.
2. Ibid., p. 176.
3. Green, T.H. quoted in R.S. Sharma's *Aspects of Political Ideas and Institute in Ancient India*, p. 1.
4. Elphinstone, M. *The History of India*, (ed.) Cowell, 9th (ed.) (1905), pp. 21–22.
5. Ibid., p. 22.
6. Davids, Rhys. *Buddhist India*, p. 1.
7. Bhandarkar, D.R., *Some Aspects of Ancient Indian Polity*, p. 163.
8. Ibid., p. 113.
9. Prasad, Beni. *The State in Ancient India*, p. 4.
10. Kane, P.V., *History of Dharmasastra*, Vol. III, p. 19.
11. Bhandarkar, D.R., op. cit., p. 69.
12. Ibid., p. 69.
13. Ibid., p. 70.
14. Ibid., pp. 70–71.
15. Quoted in V.R.R. Dikshitar's *Hindu Administrative Institutions*, p. 54.
16. Jayaswal., K.P., *Hindu Polity*, p. 342.
17. Ibid., p. 342.
18. Dikshitar, V.R.R., op. cit., p. 219.
19. Bhandarkar, D.R., op. cit., p. 16.

20. Altekar, A.S., *State and Government in Ancient India*, p. 60.
21. Ibid., p. 60.
22. Ghoshal, U.N., *A History of Indian Political Ideas*, p. 4.
23. Kane, P.V., op. cit., p. 240.
24. Bhandarkar, D.R. op. cit., p. 51.
25. Ibid., 50.
26. Prasad, Beni, op. cit., p. 513.
27. Banerjee, P.N., *Public Administration in Ancient India*, p. 39.
28. Ibid., 39.
29. Bhandarkar, D.R., op. cit., p. 132.
30. Ghoshal, U.N., op. cit., p. 540.
31. Jayaswal, K.P., op. cit., p. 185.
32. Ghoshal, U.N., op. cit., p. 538.
33. Ibid., p. 536.
34. Ibid., p. 537.
35. R.S. Sharma, op. cit., p. 352.
36. Ibid., p. 183.
37. Ibid., p. 198.
38. Ibid., p. 229.
39. Thapar, Romila., *From Lineage to State*, p. 5.
40. Ibid., p. 157.
41. R.S. Sharma, op. cit., p. 79.
42. Ibid. 86.
43. Ibid., p. 31.
44. Ibid., p. 38.
45. Ibid., p. 39.
46. Ibid., p. 41.
47. Drekmeier, Charles, *Kingship and Community in Ancient India*, p. ix.
48. Ibid., p. 251.
49. Ibid., pp. 251–252.

50. Lingat, Robert, *The Classical Law of India*, p. 218.
51. Ibid., pp. 217–218.
52. Ibid., p. 208.
53. Derrett, J.D.M., *Essays in Classical and Modern Hindu Law*, Vol. I, p. 569.
54. Ibid., p. 571.
55. Ibid., p. 571.
56. Mill, James, op. cit., pp. 182–183.
57. Jayaswal, K.P., p. 310.
58. Ibid., p. 310.
59. Ghoshal, U.N., op. cit., p. 114.
60. Ibid., p. 115.
61. Ibid., p. 115.
62. Ibid., p. 115.
63. Lingat, Robert, p. 224.
64. Ibid., p. 227.
65. Ibid., p. 228.
66. Ibid., p. 229.
67. Ibid., p. 230.
68. Ibid., p. 230.
69. Mill., James, op. cit., Vol. I, p. 202.
70. Ibid., p. 204.
71. Ibid., p. 205.
72. Ibid., p. 205.
73. Jayaswal., K.P., *Hindu Polity*, p. 322.
74. Ibid., p. 319.
75. Banerjee, P.N., *Public Administration in Ancient India*, p. 180.
76. Ghoshal, U.N., *Contributions to the History of the Hindu Revenue System*, p. 14.
77. Ibid., p. 17.
78. Altekar, A.S., op. cit., pp. 265–266.

79. Jayaswal, K.P., op. cit., p. 326.
80. Altekar, A.S., op. cit., p. 270.
81. Ibid., p. 271.
82. Ibid., p. 273.
83. Sharma, R.S., op. cit., p. 198.
84. Ibid., p. 328.
85. Ibid., p. 328.
86. Ibid., pp. 328–329.
87. Ibid., p. 329.
88. Mill, James, op. cit., p. 220.
89. Ibid., p. 221.
90. Quoted in K.P. Jayaswal's, *Hindu polity,* p. 336.
91. Jayaswal, K.P., op. cit., p. 330.
92. Altekar, A.S., op. cit., p. 227.
93. Ibid., p. 276.
94. Sharma, R.S., op. cit., p. 80.
95. Ibid., p. 81.
96. Ibid., pp. 81–82.
97. Jayaswal, K.P., op. cit., p. 329.
98. Altekar, A.S., op. cit., p. 281.
99. Ibid., p. 281.
100. Ibid., p. 284.
101. Ibid., p. 264.
102. Hall quoted in R.S. Sharma, op. cit., p. 10.
103. Viswanath, S.V., *International Relations in Ancient India,* p. 10.
104. Ibid., p. 26.
105. Ibid., p. 92.
106. Altekar, A.S., op. cit., pp. 293–294.
107. Ibid., p. 294.
108. Viswanath, S.V., op. cit., p. 110.

109. Ibid., p. 157.
110. Altekar, A.S., op. cit., p. 297.
111. Banerjee, P.N., op. cit., p. 192.
112. Ibid., p. 192.
113. Ibid., p. 193.
114. Ibid., p. 194.
115. Viswanatha, S.V., op. cit., p. 72.
116. Ibid., p. 77.
117. Ibid., pp. 25–26.
118. Sharma, R.S., op. cit., p. 394.
119. Ibid., p. 394.

6

Judicial and Penal Laws

Historians' Observations

The law books of ancient India lay great emphasis on the delivery of justice by the kings to their subjects. In the ancient Indian monarchial system, judicial powers rested with the king; but he was bound by the rules laid down by the cannons while deciding on the cases. The references of organized courts have been found from the literary and inscriptional sources. The ancient texts are replete with elaborate provisions about the administration of justice, trial procedure, evidence examination and penal laws.

Laws of Judicature

Right from the commencement of Indological studies, there has been a propensity to understand local Hindu judicial system for the administrative needs of British rulers. The earlier works by Europeans were meant primarily for judicial courts to solve the disputes among local people. In this direction, the compilation of *Vivadarnavasetu* by a group of local Bahamans, under the guidance of Governor Warren Hastings (1772–85), was a watershed development. But the credit to write comprehensively on various aspects of ancient Indian judiciary goes to James Mill. Mill, setting the tone of imperialist historiography, opined on the instruments and modes of judiciary, evidence provisions and its actual prevalence.

Mill, in the chapter entitled 'The Laws of Hindus' of his famous work *History of British India* distributes the Hindu Laws under three headings:

1. Civil Laws
2. Penal Laws
3. The Laws of Judicature

He believes that the civil and penal laws are the end while the laws of judicature are the means to that end.[1] Mill studies the laws of judicature in the sequence of its components, which he asserts, are the instruments for producing the fulfillments and the modes of using them. Mill observes that among the Hindus, the king with his Brahman assessors is the principal instrument. King being the head of the justice is an important characteristic of Hindu legal system. Explaining such a phenomenon, Mill observes that various circumstances tend to produce this arrangement. In the first place, there are hardly any laws, and he alone is entitled to judge who is entitled to legislate, since he must make a law for every occasion. In the second place, a rude people, unused to obedience would hardly respect inferior authority.[2] Mill also pronounces that the powers to legislate and amend the laws was often confined to the hands of priests. The power of legislation therefore exclusively belongs to the priesthood. The king, therefore, is so far from possessing the judicial power that he is rather the executive officer by whom the decisions of the Brahmans are carried into effect.[3]

Under the laws of Judicature, Mill has studied the rules of evidence in a greater detail. He finds that chief species of evidence, applicable to judicial cases, is the speech of witness. It is this species which makes the principal figure in the laws of Hindustan to the present age.[4] He adds that it is more than doubtful whether written evidence is at all referred to by the author of the *Ordinances of Manu*. While the evidence of speaking witness occupies a conspicuous place, the evidence of writings is entirely omitted.[5]

In Mill's opinion, some rules of evidence are good and reasonable; others are not only reverse but indicate a state of ignorance and barbarism. The different degrees of trustworthiness in different witnesses lead to mischievous rules. The most fanciful distinction surely that ever was made by an uncultivated mind is that between the father of male and the father of female offspring as a source of evidence.[6]

It is noticeable that Mill has criticized the modes of trial not only of ancient India but that of Europe also. He says that nine different modes of the trials of the Hindus (by the balance, fire, water poison, red-hot iron, etc.,) with their shocking European counterparts might consign punishment to the most innocent or save from it the most criminal of men.[7]

The above observations by Mill went on to be taken as the basic assumptions of imperialist perception of ancient Indian judiciary. Mill was followed by a number of European historians who echo his notions with some variations.

Julius Jolly devoted a full chapter to the study of ancient Indian judiciary in his book *Hindu Law and Custom*. Relying on his close observation of *Smriti*-texts and law books, he finds that the law court has been compared to human body in which the king is head, the chief judge is the mouth, the assessors are the arms, etc. More accurately, the functions of the limbs or parts of a law court, which are ten in number, are defined.[8] The king has to follow the *Dharmasutras* and the opinion of his chief judge. The council of the king is responsible together with the king himself for the injustice which the king commits by passing a wrong judgement.[9]

Jolly comments that qualification bar for the judges was set so high that it excluded absolutely *sudras* from the post of a judge.[10] Afterwards, Jolly examines the procedures, varieties and authenticity of witnesses in judicial system. He finds that the ancient Indian arbitration courts of the caste, corporations, etc., shall allow only documents as means of proof.[11] In this way, Jolly stands opposite to James Mill who insists on the entire omission of written proof in ancient Indian judicial procedure. It is noticeable that the Indologists are to some extent sympathetic while studying the institution of judiciary in ancient India and in many ways differ from imperialist notions.

With the emergence of nationalist historiography in the second half of the 19th century, not only imperialist assumptions were challenged but the study of ancient Indian judiciary was also enriched. The discovery of *Arthasastra* in 1905 by R. Shamshastri proved to be the biggest tool in the hands of nationalist historians refuting their imperialist counterparts.

K.P. Jayswal led the nationalist response profoundly in his well-known book *Hindu Polity* (1924). He asserts that the king was not arbitrary and was placed under the law. The all-powerful law, the common law of Hindus, is declared again and again to be above the king and as the king of kings.[12] Jayswal asserted, 'The administration of justice under Hindu Monarchy remained always separate from the executive, and generally independent in form and ever independent in spirit. The reason for this was that it was the lawyers who were appointed judges and lawyers as a rule were from amongst the Brahmins (not kshatriya).'[13] Jayswal throws light on the judicial set-up in ancient India. He says, 'Then law court bore the ancient Vedic name, the *sabha* .... The judges were always helped by the community in administration of justice. They made up the *sabha* and were, to quote a modern word, the jury of court.'[14] 'Their number was odd, to provide for voting and it was enjoined on them to speak according to law. A jury which kept its mouth shut or spoke what is not *dharma* was considered immoral.'[15]

In his view, the jury members are the 'examiners of the cause while the judge, their president the "speaker" and the king as carrying out the punishment'.[16] He, taking the references from *Mrichchkatika* and Buddhist *Jatakas*, has asserted that the purity of justice, real rule of law and impartial justice delivery were the routine business of ancient Indian judiciary.[17]

The lead given by Jayswal was followed by many Indian scholars, namely, P.N. Sen and P.V. Kane. Sen studied the laws of judicature and evidence entitled in the chapter entitled 'Adjective Law' in his book *The General Principles of Hindu Jurisprudence* (1918). He has described in full detail the constitution of courts and qualifications for the judges. Though he has not commented categorically on the exclusion of *sudras* from being appointed as judges but noted, 'Besides the councilors selected and appointed by the king ... it was declared that other versed in the law who attend the court should, if occasion arises, give their own opinion on a disputed point of law to prevent a perversion of justice.'[18] He calls such intervening lawyers as '*amicus curiae*' and observes that his 'post ended when he gave out his opinion, and it was no part of his business to remonstrate with the king if he did not want to follow'.[19]

Opining on the gradation of courts, Sen points out that families, corporations, and communities were also charged with the decision of judicial proceedings.[20] However, 'these local courts had a sort of delegated authority within their limited spheres, but their decisions were subject to appeal'.[21] Besides, Sen has described judicial procedure involving modes of lodging a complaint and summoning of defendant. He regards the imposing of legal restraint (*asedha*) a 'peculiar procedure recognized by Hindu law to ensure the attendance of a defendant'.[22] Legal restraint, which could be so imposed, was fourfold: local, temporary, inhibition from going abroad, and from the pursuit of particular work or occupation.[23]

Sen has elaborated the provisions of evidence in Hindu law. He writes, 'Evidence is said to consist of documents, possession and witness; in absence of all these, a divine test is presented.[24] Earlier James Mill has condemned the divine test or ordeals in deciding the litigious disputes. But Sen speaks of the 'exceptional' practice of ordeals. He observes,

> 'When one adduces human evidence and the other appeals to divine test, the king will proceed to examine the human evidence, and will not have recourse to divine test. A decision by divine test is allowable only in the absence of human evidence.'[25]

P.V. Kane, in the volume 3 of his work *History of Dharmasastra* presented a detailed study of ancient Indian judiciary. He has described various types of *Vyavahara* (law-suit or dispute in a court' and legal procedure) found in *Manusmrit* (18) *Kautilya* (16). *Yajnavalkya* (20). He analyses the matters for *kantak-sodhana* courts by *Kautilya* and observes that the number of offences dealt with by Kautilya was very large and his treatment in some respects compared favorably with such modern criminal codes as the Indian Penal Code.[26] Relying on many references, Kane asserts the prevalence of written document as a proof in the courts. Commenting on the disqualification of women as witness, he says that Ancient Hindu law is not singular in its partial rejection of the testimony of women, and he finds it a little better than the Ancient Roman Law or the medieval European laws which excluded entirely the testimony of women.[27]

The nationalist line of writing was further buttressed by a number of indigenous scholars who not only challenged the imperialist vision of ancient Indian judiciary, but also revealed its new dimensions. H.N. Tripathi has studied the administration of justice, its aims, development, types of judiciary and judges, etc., in full detail in his book *Prachin Bharat me Rajya aur Nyaypalika*. He observes that in the Vedic period *sabha* and *samiti* functioned as judicial bodies and the king was not supreme. Though intermediary in the administration of justice but later up to the period of *Smritis*, the king emerged as the head of judicial set up and his assembly as the highest court.[28] Contrary to the imperialist assumption, he says, that judicial administration was based not on individual choice but on laws accepted by society and state. The king was the ultimate source of judicial powers but could not voluntarily conduct the judiciary. It was necessary for him to consult the *pradvivaka* (chief justice) and other court members, while announcing the judgements.[29]

Shraddhakar Supakar in his book *The Law of Evidence in Ancient India* (1990) has discussed the necessity of evidences and its types: witness (*sakshi*), documents (*alekhya*), possession (*bhukti*) and ordeals (*divya*) and other related issues. He says that the problem of proof arises in the third stage of litigation, i.e., after (a) *bhasha* (plaint or complaint) and (b) *uttar* (reply or defence).[30] Third and fourth stage comprised *kriyapad* (proof examinitaion) and *sadhyasiddhi* (decree/verdict) respectively. The four layers of judicial procedures is termed '*chatushpad*' in law books. Elaborate rules are laid-down regarding the evidence of witness. The most fundamental rule is the exclusion of hearsay evidences from the time of Manu and even earlier.[31]

Supakar has viewed the *Yukti* of *Smriti* texts as proof of circumstantial evidence and compared it with similar Muslim and modern law.[32]

No study of the subject will be complete without mentioning the Marxist interpretation of ancient Indian judiciary. R.S. Sharma leads this school of thought in studying the adjective laws of ancient India. He furnishes a critical survey of different phases of judiciary in ancient India. Like many scholars, he accepts that *sabha* was judicial body in Vadic period. He opines, 'We have, therefore, no doubt that the sabha had judicial functions to discharge, although most references to this aspect belong to later Vedic times. In any case Jayaswal's statement that the *sabha* was a national judicature is not sound, for there may have been several clan *sabhas*.'[33]

Prof. Sharma traces the prevalence of caste element in ancient Indian judiciary. He claims that the early state was a superstructure raised on relations existing between the four social orders which hindered one of the primary functions of the state, i.e., providing justice.[34] He remarks, 'In fact the effect of the *varna* system is to be seen most clearly in the organization of the judicial system and the legislation framed by Brahmanical law-givers. Judges were to be recruited on caste basis. *Manu* and *Yajnavalkya* give the first preferences to Brahman; failing them, members of the next two classes could be appointed judges, but on no account could a sudra be permitted to hold this office.'[35]

Prof. Sharma has highlighted the existence of class-legislation in the law of evidence. He notes, 'To begin with the law of evidence, the outcaste, one fallen from his varna duties, could not act as a witness and members of one caste could not act as a witness for persons of the other castes.'[36] 'It was further provided that *dasas* (slaves) or *bhritkas* (servants), obviously recruited from sudra varna, must not be examined as witness.'[37] 'While deposing, members of different castes were to be administered different kinds of oath and shown different kinds of treatment. The same discrimination obtained in matters of ordeals. Yajnavalkya lays down the ordeals of weight, fire, water, and poison, respectively for the four *varnas*.'[38]

It is noticeable that R.S. Sharma's analysis of adjective laws and evidence is sometime similar to that of imperialists, but the former's methodology of research is materialistic. For example, Prof. Sharma studies the judicial administration of Gupta period in the light of expanding trends of land grants and feudal elements. He remarks, 'On account of the growth of private property in land which was sold for money in Gupta period we find very detailed laws about partition, sale, mortgage and lease of land in Gupta law books. All this shows considerable progress of rational trends, but curiously enough superstitions invade the judicial procedure.'[39] Manu prescribes only two types of ordeal, Yajnavalkya and Narada raise the number to five, and Brihspati to nine.[40]

The other distinct feature of judiciary in Gupta period as underlined by Prof. Sharma is a hierarchy of local courts, which are to be recognized but not established by the king.[41] Apart from mentioning many grades of local courts such as *kula, sreni* and *puga*, law books advise farmers, artisans, and traders, etc., to form their own courts. On this Prof. Sharma comments 'Professional associations functioned as courts of justice, which obviated the necessity of providing justice through the state machinary.'[42] These observations are consistent with Sharma's much discussed hypothesis of the feudalization of polity.

From the above survey, it becomes clear that the adjective and evidence laws of ancient India underwent innumerable interpretations in modern historiography. Particular tool of interpretation chosen by particular historians facilitated the countless divergent views of the subject. In this situation, it is difficult to give a universally acceptable generalization on the instant topic. Yet, it can be safely argued that judiciary in ancient India did not have a uniform pattern. In respect to time and space, it too went changing. Regarding the administration of justice, qualifications of judges, hierarchy of courts, ordeals, evidence-provisions, etc., there are elaborate and subtle provisions in ancient Indian law books. But no one can deny wholly the existence of caste- and gender-related bias in judicial matters. At most, there can be different interpretations or even justifications, but the facts remain there. So a critical, comprehensive and holistic approach is required to view the institution of judiciary in ancient India.

Penal Laws

An offence is the breach of any existing law. In early Indian law books, we come across various types of offences involving different types of punishments. In modern jurisprudence, the main theories of punishments are 'retributive, 'deterrent' or 'preventive' and 'reformative'. But in ancient Indian perspective, all theories can be categorized as worldly forms of punishment. *Dharmasastras* provided for spiritual punishment or expiation as well in respect to many sinful acts.

The European historians initiated the modern studies on the laws of offences and punishment in ancient India. James Mill maintains that two principles – severity and retaliation – universally characterize the penal code of a barbarous people.[43] Turning to the Indian scenario, he observes, 'Notwithstanding the mildness which has generally been attributed to the Hindu character, hardly any nation is distinguished for more sanguinary laws'.[44] Referring to William Jones' statement, he claims that 'the cruel mutilations practised by native powers are shocking to humanity'.[45]

James Mill has pointed out caste discrimination in the provisions of offences and punishments and condemned them sternly. He says, 'With regard to offences committed by individuals of different ranks, it is rare, even among the rudest people, to find the principle of unequal punishments, expressly avowed; and comparative impunity granted by law to the crimes of the great.'[46] He adds, 'Among the Hindus, whatever be the crime committed, if it is by a Brahman, the punishment is in general comparatively slight; if by a *shudra* it is violent and cruel. For all the more serious accusations against any of the superior orders, the punishment of the *shudra* is far more dreadful'.[47]

Besides, Mill has discussed the various 'principal acts erected into punishable offences' by the Hindu law such as false witness or perjury, defamation, assault, theft, outrage, adultery, etc. He opined that adultery is a very complicated subject and in the Hindu language it includes every unlawful species of sexual indulgence, from the least, to the most injurious, or offensive.[48] He explained this trend with the general status of women in East. He remarks, 'In accordance with the general spirit of Eastern nations, among whom an extraordinary value is set on the chastity of the women, it's more aggravated violations are punished by the most shocking dealt which human cruelty has probably devised, that of burning on a heated plate of iron.'[49]

Mill's above-mentioned assumptions came to be regarded as cliché by a number of imperialist historians. Sir Henry Sumner Maine (*Ancient Law*, 1866) added many new conceptual frameworks to study the ancient laws on crime and punishment. He observers that 'the penal law of ancient communities is not the law of crimes; it is the law of wrongs, or, to use the English technical word, of torts.[50] The person injured proceeds against the wrong-doer by an ordinary civil action, and recovers compensation in the shape of money, if he succeeds.[51] This view implicitly involves the absence of criminal jurisprudence in beginning of Indian law. In his findings, 'the evolution of criminal law begins with the understanding that the conception of crime is distinguished from that of wrong or tort, and from that of sin, to the idea of injury to the state or collective community.'[52]

Julius Jolly further enriched the historiography of the subject. He opines that the expressions for the general concept of 'crime, transgressions' are very numerous, but are mostly of a religious nature, such as, *agha, pap, asubh*, etc.[53] The derived words *atipataka, mahptaka, anupataka*, signifying the 'crimes which cause the loss of caste', are especially important because they exhibit the close connection between criminal law and the caste system.[54]

According to Jolly, penances (*prayaschita*) were designed for Brahmans' benefit. He writes, 'As old as the lists of sins is the theory of penances, the determination and prescription of which was one of the most essential means of maintaining the influence of the Brahmans and frequently was also a lucrative source of income for them.'[55] He finds it also that 'the graver the sins the more difficult are the penances; for this reason a deadly sin may be expiated for only by suicide.[56]

Regarding the relation between spiritual and worldly punishments, Jolly disputes Burnell's view that the secular criminal law is of later origin. Instead, he says, 'On the whole the two systems of punishment had developed independently of each other .... Nothing stood in the way to prevent the welding together of spiritual and worldly punishments and the punished criminal moreover performed also the penances prescribed in the *Dharmasutras* in order to gain re-admission into his caste.'[57] However, treading a general imperialist path, he maintains that in both of these systems the caste distinction and the privileges of the Brahman have been fully recognized which stand out prominently particularly in the punishments and penances for murder, maiming, adultery, theft, injuries and other grave crimes.[58]

Jolly identifies the ten chief crimes of *Smritis* with the *Dasaparadha* mentioned in certain inscriptions. He holds the view that institution of blood-money betrays a primitive society and later in its place, punishments, partly secular and partly spiritual in character came in vogue.[59] He believes that forced labour, too, appears as a public punishment as in working off a debt and punishment by imprison is rather rarely mentioned in ancient works.[60]

Nationalists led by P.N. Sen responded to the imperialist formulations on Hindu law of offences and punishment. Sen in the chapter, 'The Law of the Torts and the Law of Crimes' of his book, countered Maine's view that the penal law of ancient communities was not the law of crimes but of wrongs or 'torts'. He (Sen) observes that 'in Hindu Law punishments of crimes occupied a more prominent place than the compensation for wrongs; ... and the compensation was generally levied in addition to and not in substitution for the penalty which it was considered to be the duty of the king to impose'.[61] He concludes, 'It may, therefore, be safely pronounced that the penal law of the Hindus was the law of crimes in the strict sense, and the law of torts occupied a comparatively subordinate and less important position in that system.'[62]

The issue of caste considerations in Hindu law of punishment has dominated imperialist historiography on the subject. Sen tries to explain the caste distinctions 'having regard to the peculiar organization of the ancient Hindu society'. He observes,

> 'This (caste distinctions) may to some extent be accounted for on the ground that in cases where insult or indignity was a constituent element of the offence, the punishment was to be severe when the delinquent belonged to a lower caste in relation to the complainant, for the outrage proceeding from the former against the latter made the insult more keenly felt and consequently deserved to be put down with a heavier punishment.'[63]

He adds, 'However, it would be a mistake to suppose that this was the universal rule and that for every offence punishment increased in severity according to the inferiority of caste of the culprit.'[64]

Contrasting the situation, Sen states that 'in cases where the offence was an outcome of moral depravity, but did not involve insult to the complainant as an element to be taken into consideration in measuring the enormity of the crime, a person belonging to a higher caste who had less excuse for the same was generally imposed a heavier punishment'.[65] He has substantiated this point with a reference from *Manu* (8, 337–338) where a Brahman, knowing what is right and what is wrong is punished sixty-four times to that of the ignorant Shudra for the theft. Finally, he concludes, 'The Hindu Law cannot, therefore, be accused of showing unmixed or unqualified partiality towards people belonging to higher caste in the administration of criminal justice.'[66] It is to be mentioned that Sen himself has noted that he doesn't try to justify the caste factor, determining the measures of punishment.[67]

P.V. Kane like Sen contradicts Maine's view: 'Penal Law of ancient communities is not the law of crimes but ... of torts.' He (Kane) says, 'The king could of his own motion take cognizance of many wrongs called *chalas, padas* and *aparadhas* and it is very clear that in such crimes as theft, assault, adultery, rape and manslaughter, the *smriti* texts do not prescribe only a money compensation to the person wronged, but corporal punishment in the first instance and monetary compensation in addition.'[68]

Kane explains the provisions of 'retaliation' in the laws of punishment, in the light of victims' sentiment. He writes, 'The person wronged feels a great urge for revenge or retaliation and other men sympathize with that emotion. The individual, however, could not, in civilized societies, take the law into his own hands; therefore the state saw to it that the emotion for retaliation or revenge was to some degree satisfied by the adequate punishment of the wrongdoer.'[69]

Kane observes gradual improvement in the amount of 'severity' in ancient Indian punishment. He notes, 'It will be seen from the early *sutras* like that of *Gautam* and from the *Manusmrti* that the more ancient criminal law in India was very severe and drastic, but that from the times of Yajnavalkya, Narada and Brihaspati, the rigour of punishments was lessened and softened and fines came to be the ordinary punishments for many crimes, as is noted by Fa Hien (399–414 AD) in relation to middle India (*Madhadesa*) under the Guptas apparently.'[70]

Regarding the much-discussed exemption of Brahmans from corporal and death punishment, Kane believes that it was not unanimous and universal rule.[71] He has quoted many references from *Kautilya* (IV, 11), *Mricchakatika* and *Katyayana* (806 AD) which indicate death sentences provided for Brahmans in certain conditions.[72]

The laws pertaining to crime and punishment were further studied by Prof. N.C. Tyagi (*The Judiciary and Judicial Process in Ancient India,* published in *Political, Legal and Military History of India,* Vol. I, (H.S. Bhatiya, ed, Delhi, 1984) Chakradhar Jha (*History and Sources of Law in Ancient India*, New Delhi, 1987), and many others. Chakradhar Jha proclaimed that in ancient India, since the time of the Vedas, there was a well-defined demarcating line of civil and criminal law.[73] He says, 'Though in the *Vedas* and in the *Dharma Sutra* distinct headings for civil disputes and criminal offences are not traceable; but there was very clear demarcating line of the two nature of disputes.'[74]

Prof. R.S. Sharma emphasized the elements of class legislation in the provisions for punishments also. He says, 'Like the code of Hammurabi or the Anglo-Saxon code, the *Dharmasastras* prescribe different punishments for different varnas for the same offence. The value of the compensatory fine in the case of death varies from caste to caste.'[75] He finds that between the beginnings of such discriminatory laws with the early law books and their climax with Manu, Kautilya's legislation introduces a liberal interlude, its object being to provide a scheme of imperial laws overriding petty considerations of caste.[76]

Sharma says, 'In consonance with his view that moderation is the essence of the administration of justice, Kautilya tries to lessen the rigours of class legislation. According to him in certain cases capital punishment could be inflicted even upon the Brahmans. For giving false evidence he possibly prescribes the same fine for members of all castes'.[77] Like P.V. Kane, he too admits the softening of discriminatory punishments in Gupta period, 'leading to some improvement in the legal status of the fourth varna'; but he explains this change materialistically.[78]

Thus, above survey of reflections on the institution of justice delivery reveals plenty of approaches to understand it in ancient Indian context. But almost all of them effuse certain prejudices and pre-conceived principles, be it imperialism, nationalism or Marxism. Imperialists and Marxists more than often appear close in criticizing the caste considerations in adjective and penal laws of early India, while nationalists try to either defend or generalize such provisions. It is some legal historians of post-modern period like Robert Lingat and J.D.M. Derrett who seem to adopt a more incisive and holistic approach.

Regarding the much-discussed issue of 'torts' and 'crimes', Lingat says that the general evolution of criminal law tends to substitute crimes for torts, to take away satisfaction of vengeance from the victims in order to transfer that concern to state. He further remarks, 'Hindu law never followed out that evolution completely and the victim of a tort is often allowed to claim, personally, that penalties should be imposed on the alleged tortfeasor. But the penalties are inflicted by the state; when a fine is in question that passes, as a general rule, to the king'.[79] He adds, 'On the other hand it is not rare for the tort, irrespective of the sanctions relative to it in private law, to figure equally amongst the matters which the king may take cognizance of on his own initiative.'[80] Finally, he concludes, 'Instead of the substitution of a crime for a tort – which would mark the end of the evolution of the law – we are confronted by two parallel solutions, not conceived of as cumulative'.[81]

Like P.N. Sen and R.S. Sharma, Lingat too accepts the existence of a series of local courts – *kula, sreni, gana* or *puga* – but he notes that their jurisdictions are probably of customary origin, and the *dharma-sastras* only confirm their existence, submitting them to the king's control. They do not administer justice by virtue of delegation from the king but by virtue of their own power which is originally attached to the very existence of the body itself'.[82] Lingat opines that the king's court is the only court which is dealt with by the *dharma-sastra*, the only one for which their rules relative to the composition of the tribunal, the procedure or even the deciding of cases really apply.[83]

Similarly, Derrett in his article 'The Role of Jurists in Ancient Indian Law' favoured a more plausible view. He remarked, 'Since *smritis* differed considerably from each other in many places, and since the same continuous *Smriti* might contain contradictions, the task of reconciling the divergent *smritis* was the foremost task of the jurists. When this was done there was no question of going back to the literal meaning of any particular *smriti*.'[84] Thus, interpretations of Lingant and Derrett are not swept by any sweeping generalization and are often free from imperialist stereotypes. They deduce their conclusions based on original text and judge it in its totality.

Notes

1. Mill, James, *The History of British India,* I, P. 187.
2. Ibid., pp. 182–83.
3. Ibid., p. 188.
4. Ibid., p. 188.

5. Ibid., pp. 188–89.
6. Ibid., p. 189.
7. Ibid., p. 194–95.
8. Jolly, J., *Hindu law and Custom*, p. 287.
9. Ibid., p. 286.
10. Ibid., p. 289.
11. Ibid., p. 308.
12. Jayaswal, K.P., *Hindu Polity*, p. 152
13. Ibid., p. 153.
14. Ibid., p. 154.
15. Ibid., p. 312.
16. Ibid., p. 314.
17. Ibid., p. 314.
18. Sen, P.N., *The General Principles of Hindu Jurisprudence*, p. 362.
19. Ibid., p. 363.
20. Ibid., p. 363.
21. Ibid., p. 363.
22. Ibid., p. 365.
23. Ibid., p. 366.
24. Ibid., p. 371.
25. Ibid., p. 371.
26. P.V. Kane, *History of Dharmasastra*, Vol. III, p. 257
27. Ibid., P. 338.
28. H.N. Tripathi, *Pracheen Bharat mein Rajya aur Nyaypalika*, p. 120.
29. Ibid., p. 121.
30. Supakar, Shraddhakar, *The Law of Evidence in Ancient India*, p. xvii.
31. Ibid., p. xviii.
32. Ibid., pp. xx–xxi.

33. Sharma, R.S., *Aspects of Political Ideas and Institutions in Ancient India*, p. 109.
34. Ibid., p. 243.
35. Ibid., pp. 243–244.
36. Ibid., p. 244.
37. Ibid., p. 244.
38. Ibid., p. 244.
39. Ibid., p. 337.
40. Ibid., p. 337.
41. Ibid., p. 338.
42. Ibid., p. 339.
43. Mill, James, op. cit., p. 176.
44. Ibid., p. 176.
45. Ibid., pp. 177–178.
46. Ibid., p. 181.
47. Ibid., p. 181.
48. Ibid., p. 186.
49. Ibid., p. 187.
50. Maine, Sir Henry, *Ancient Law*, p. 328.
51. Ibid., p. 328.
52. Ibid., p. 341.
53. Jolly., J., op. cit., p. 251.
54. Ibid., p. 251.
55. Ibid., p. 255.
56. Ibid., p. 258.
57. Ibid., p. 263.
58. Ibid., p. 264.
59. Ibid., p. 275.
60. Ibid., p. 282.
61. Sen, P.N., op. cit., p. 335.
62. Ibid., p. 336.

63. Ibid., p. 346.
64. Ibid., p. 346.
65. Ibid., pp. 346–347.
66. Ibid., p. 347.
67. Ibid., p. 349.
68. Kane, P.V., op. cit., p. 387.
69. Ibid., p. 388.
70. Ibid., p. 390.
71. Ibid., p. 398.
72. Ibid., pp. 398–399.
73. Jha, Chakradhar., *History and Sources of Law in Ancient India*, p. 210.
74. Ibid., p. 210.
75. Sharma, R.S., op. cit., 245.
76. Ibid., p. 246.
77. Ibid., p. 246.
78. Ibid., p. 245.
79. Lingat, Robert, *The Classical Law of India*, p. 245.
80. Ibid., pp. 244–245.
81. Ibid., p. 245.
82. Ibid., p. 246.
83. Ibid., p. 248.
84. Derrett, J.D.M., *Essays in Classical and Modern Hindu Law*, Vol. I, p. 216.

Bibliography

Primary Sources

Apasthambh Dharmshutra, (ed.) G. Buhlar, Government Central Book Depot, Bombay, 1892–94.

Arthashastra of Kautilya, (ed.) R. Shamshatry. Mysore, 1924.

Baudhayan Grhyashutra, (ed.) R. Shamshatry, Oriental Library Publication, University of Mysore, 1920.

Brahaspati Smriti, (ed.) K.V. Rangaswai Aiyangar, Baroda, 1941.

Digh Nikaya (Hindi), Tr. Rahul Sanskrityayan and Jagadis Kashyap, Banaras 1936.

Kamandakiya Nitisar, (ed.) Rajendra Lal Mitra, Calcutta, 1884.

Manu Smriti or Manav Dharmshashtra, (ed.) S.N. Mandlik, Ganapati Krishnaji Press, Bombay, 1886, Tr. G. Buhlar, Sacred Book of East series (hereafter SBE), xxv, Oxford, 1886.

Narad Smriti with extracts from the commentary of *Asahaya,* (ed.) J. Jolly, Calcutta, 1885. Tr. J. Jolly, SBE, xxxiii Oxford, 1889.

Vinaya Pitak, (The *Book of Discipline),* Tr. I.B. Horner, Oxford, London, 1938–52.

Vishnu Smriti or Vaishnav Dharmashashtra, (with commentary of Nanda Padit called *Vaijayanti*), (ed.) J. Jolly, Calcutta, 1881.

Yajnavalkya Smriti with Virmitrodaya and Mitakshara, Chaukhambha Sanskrit Series, Banaras, 1930.

Secondary Sources

Agrawal, Rajkumari. *Matrimonial Remedies under Hindu Law*, N.M. Tripathi Pvt. Ltd. Bombay, 1976.

Aiyer, C.P. Ramaswami. *Indian Political Theories*, Madras, 1937.

——. *The Philosophical Basis of Indian Legal and Social Systems*, Madras, 1949.

Aiyangar, K.V. Rangaswami., *Aspects of Social and Political Systems of Manusmriti*, Lucknow, 1949.

——. *Some Aspects of Ancient Indian Polity*, Madras, 1935.

——. *Rajdharma*, Madras, 1941.

——. *Some Aspects of Hindu View of Life according to DharmaÑ~stra*, Baroda, 1952.

Aiyer, Narayan, R.A. *The History of the Hindu Law in the Vedic Age and in the Post-Vedic times down to the Institute of Manu*, Madras, 1925.

Ali, B. Sheik. *History: Its Theory and Method*, Macmillan, Madras, 1978.

Altekar, A.S. *State and Government in Ancient India*, Banaras, 1949.

——. *Sources of Hindu Dharma*, Institute of Public Administration, Sholapur, 1952.

Ambedkar, B.R. *Writings and Speeches*, Vol. 4, 1978, Vol. 5, 1989, Education Dept, Govt. of Maharastra, Bombay.

Anderson, Perry. *Lineages of Absolutist State*, New Left Books, Verso; London, 1974.

——. *Passages from Antiquity to Feudalism*, London, 1974.

Anjaria, H.G. *Nature and Grounds of Political Obligations in the Hindu State*, London, 1935.

Apte, V.M. *Social and Religious Life in the Griha Sutras*, Bombay, 1954.

Aron, R. *Philosophy of History*, Paris, 1950.

Austin, John. *Lectures on Jurisprudence*, London, 1920.

Ayyar, Nataraja. *Mimansa Jurisprudence*, Ganganath Research Institute, Alld, 1952.

Baikar, H. and H. *Family, Marriage & Parenthood*, Boston, 1948

Banerjee, S.C. *Dharma – Sutra, A Study in their Origin and Development*, Calcutta, 1962.

Bandopadhaya, N.C. *Development of Hindu Polity and Political Theories*, Calcutta, 1927.

——. *Kautilya or an Exposition of His Social and Political Theory*, Calcutta, National Publishing House, 1927.

Bandopadhyaya, S.C. Smriti-sastre Bangali, Calcutta, 1962.

Banerji, G.D. *Hindu Law of Marriage and Stridhan*, Calcutta, 1923.

Banerjee, P.N. *Public Administration in Ancient India*, London, Macmillian, 1916.

——. *International Law and Custom in Ancient India*, Reprint from Journal of Department of Letters, xx, Calcutta University, 1920.

——. *A History of Indian Taxation*, London, 1930.

Barker, Earnest. *The Political Thought of Plato and Aristotle*, New York, Putnam, 1906.

——. *Church, State and Study*, London, Methuen, 1930.

Basham, A.L. *The Wonder That was India*, London, Sidewick & Jackson, 1954.

Basu, D.D. and Akbar, H.K., *Hindu Vidhi*, Allahabad, 2000.

Basu, P. *Indo-Aryan Polity*, London, 1925.

Beard, C.A. *The Economic Basis of Politics*, New York, 1945.

Beteille, Andre. *Society and Polity in India: Essays in a Comparative Perspective*, Delhi Oxford University Press, 1997.

Bhandarkar, D.R. *Some Aspects of Ancient Hindu Polity*, Varanasi, 1929.

——. *Some Aspects of Ancient Indian Culture*, Madras, 1940.

Bhatiya, H.S. ed. *Political, Legal and Military History of India* Vol. I and II. New Delhi, 1984.

Bhattacharya, Chanchal A. *The Concept of Theft in Classical Hindu Law*, New Delhi, 1990.

Bhattacharya, J. *Commentaries on the Hindu Law*, Calcutta, 1909.

Bhattacharya, K.K. *The Law Relating to Joint Family*, Calcutta, 1885.

Bhattacharya, S.C. 'Political Authority and Brahman Kshatriya Relationship in Early India-An Aspect of the Power Elite Configuration', *Indian Historical Review*, Vol. 10, No. 1–2, 1984, pp. 1–20.

——. 'Toynbee on Ancient India', *Journal of Indian History*, Vol. XLIV, part II, 1966, pp. 367–396.

Birendra, Nath. *Judicial Administration in Ancient India*, Patna, 1979

Block, Marc, *Feudal Society*, London, 1961; trans. L.A. Manyon, Chicago, 1964.

Bloomfield, M. *Religion of the Veda*, New York, 1908.

Bosanquet, Bernard. *The Philosophical Theory of the State*, London, Macmillan, 1920.

Bougle, C. *Essays on the Caste System*, trans. D. Pocock, Cambridge, 1953.

Buckland, W.W. *Some Reflections on Jurispreudence*, Cambridge, U.P. 1945.

Bury J.B. *Idea of Progress*, (First published, 1932) New York, 1955.

Cahn, Edmund N. *Sense of Injustice, An Anthromorphic view of Law*, New York, 1949.

Carr, E.H. *What is History?*, Alfred A. Knopf, New York, 1964.

Cassirer, Earnest, *The Myth of the State*, Garden City, N.Y., Anchor Paperback, 1955.

Chakravarti, C. *A Study in Hindu Social Polity*, Calcutta, 1923.

Chakravarti, P.C. *The Art of War in Ancient India*, Dacca, 1941.

Chakravarti, Uma. *Gendering Caste: Through a Feminist Lens*, Kolkata, 2006.

Chanana, D. *Slavery in Ancient India*, New Delhi, 1960.

Chatterjee, H.L. *International Law and Inter-State Relations in Ancient India*, Calcutta, 1958.

Chaudhary, R.K. *Ancient Indian Law and Justice*, Banaras, 1953.

Classen, H.J.M. and Skalnik, P, (ed). *The Early State*, Mouton, The Hague, 1978.

Cohen, R. and E.R. Service (ed). *Origins of the State*, Philadelphia, 1978.

Colebrooke, H.T. *Miscellaneous Essays*, (ed.) E.B. Cowell, Higgin Botham, London, 1871–72.

Collingwood, R.G. *The Idea of History*, (ed. T.M. Knox, First pub., 1946) London, 1966.

Coomaraswamy, Anand. 'Hindu Theory of State and Social Compact,' *Hindustan Review*, May–June, 1918.

——. *Spiritual Authority and Temporal Power in the Indian Theory of Government*, New Haven 1942.

Coulborn, Rushton, (ed.) *Feudalism in History*, Princeton, 1956.

Cox, Oliver Cromwell. *Caste, Class, and Race*. New York, 1948.

Damle, Y.B. *Caste: A review of the Literature on Caste*, M.I.T. 1961.

Dange, S.A. *India from Primitive Communism to Slavery*, Bombay, PPH, 1949.

Danto, Arthur Coleman. *Analytical Philosophy of History*, Cambridge U.P. 1965.

Das, Babu Bhagavan. *The Science of Social Organization, or the Laws of Manu*, 2nd edn. Madras, 1935.

Dasupta, Rasmprasad. *Crime and Punishment in Ancient India*, Calcutta, 1930.

Date, G.T. *The Art of War in Ancient India*, London, 1929.

Davar, R.S. and K.D.P. Madan. *General Principles of Indian Law*, Bombay, 1950.

Davis, Donald R. Jr. *The Spirit of Hindu Law*, Cambridge University Press, 2010.

Derrett, J.D.M. *Hindu Law, Past and present*, Calcutta, 1957.

——. *Religion, Law and the State in India*, London, 1968.

——. *Essays in Classical and Modern Hindu Law*, Leiden, 1977.

——. The Death of a Marriage Law, Delhi, 1978.

——. *Dharmasutra, Apastamba Dharmasutra*, (ed.) G. Buhler, B.S.S., 1892–4.

——. (The Sacred Laws of the Aryas). trans. G. Buhler, (ed.) M. Muller, S.B.E., Vol. xiv, Oxford, 1882.

——. *Gautam Dharmasutra*, ed G.S. Gokhale, Anandasrama Sanskrit Series, Poona, 1910.

——. ('The Sacred Laws of the Aryas'), trans. G. Buhler, (ed.) M. Muller, *S.B.E.*, Vol. II, Oxford, 1879.

——. Vashishtha Dharmasutra, (ed.) A.A. Futher Bombay, 1916.

——. ('The Sacred Laws of the Aryas'), trans. G. Buhler, (ed.) M. Muller, *S.B.E.*, Vol. xiv, Oxford, 1882.

Diamond, A.S. *Primitive Law*, London, 1935.

Diksit, Premmumari. *Mahabharata men Rajyavyavastha*, Lucknow, Archana Prakashan, 1970.

Dikshitar, V.R.R. *The Gupta Polity*, University of Madras, 1952.

——. *Hindu Administrative Institutions*, University of Madras, 1929.

——. *Mauryan Polity*, University of Madra, 1932.

——. *War in Ancient India*, 2nd (ed.) Madras, 1948.

Diwan, Paras. *Modern Hindu Law: Codified and Uncodified*, Allahabad, 1972.

Dray, William. *Philosophy of History*, 1964.

Drekmeier, Charles. *Kingship and Community in Early India*, California, Stanford University Press, 1962.

Dubey, Prof. Sitaram. ed. *Social Ideals and Reality in Ancient India*, Jaipur, RBSA Publishers, 2017.

Dubois, Abbe Jean Astoine. *Hindu Manners,* Customs and Ceremonies (Trans. H.K. Beauchamp), Oxford U.P. 1897.

Dumount, L. *Homo Hierarchicus*, Paris, 1966; trans., London, 1972.

——. 'The Conception of Kingship in Ancient India', CIS, Vol. 6, 1962, pp. 407–77.

Dunning, W.A. *Political Theories, Ancient and Médieval*, New York, Macmillan, 1902.

Dutt, N.K. *The Aryanisation of India*, Calcutta, 1925.

——. *Origin and Growth of Caste in India*, London, 1921.

Dutta, B.N. *Hindu Law of Inheritance*, Calcutta, 1957.

——. *Studies in Indian Social Polity*, Calcutta, 1944.

Dutta, R.C. *Early Hindu Civilization*, Punthi Pustak, Calcutta, 1888.

Elliot, Sir Henry M. and J. Dowson. (ed). *The History of India as Told by Its Historians*, 8 vols. London, 1867–77: Calcutta, 1953.

Elphinstone, Montsturat. *The History of India* 9th (ed.) London, 1905.

Engles, F. *The Origin of the Family, Private Property and the State*, Moscow, 1948

Fortes, M. *Kinship and the Social Order*, Chicago, 1969.

Frankfort, H. *Kingship and the Gods*, Chicago, 1948.

Fried, Morton H. *The Evolution of Political Society*, New York, 1967.

Gadd, C.J. *Ideas of Divine Rule in the Ancient East*, London, 1948.

Gardner, P. *Theories of History*, Illinois, 1959.

Gaur, Hari Singh. *The Hindu Code*, Nagpur, 1938.

Gettell, R.G. *History of Political Thought*, New York, 1924.

Gharpure, J.C. *Hindu Law*, 4th edn. Bombay. 1931.

——. *Rights of Women Under the Hndu law*, Bombay 1944.

Ghose, Jogendra Chandra. *Principles of Hindu Law*, Calcutta, 1906.

Ghoshal, U.N. *Contribution to the History of Hindu Revenue System*, Sarswat Library, Calcutta, 1929.

——. *A History of Hindu Public Life*, Ramesh Ghoshal Calcutta, 1945, ii (*A History of Indian Public Life*), OUP, Bombay, 1966.

——. *A History of Indian Political Ideas*, Bombay, OUP, 1959. Originally published as in 1923 as *Hindu Political Theories*.

——. *The Beginnings of Indian Historiography and other Essays*, Calcutta, 1944.

Ghurye, G.S. *Caste and Race in India*, New York, 1932.

Godelier, M. *Perspectives in Marxist Anthropology*, Cambridge, 1977.

Gonda, Jan. *Ancient Indian Kingship from Religious Point of view*, E.J. Brill, Leiden 1969.

Gopalkrishnan, T.P. *Codified Hindu Law*, Allahabad, 1962.

Goyal, P.C. *Effect of Hindu Succession Act, 1956 on Direct Taxation of Mitakshara Hindus*, Allahabad, 1978.

Guha, R. *Subaltren Studies*, OVP, Delhi.

Gunawardan, R.A.L.H. 'The Analysis of Pre-Colonial Social Foundation in Asia in the writings of Karl Marx, *Indian Historical Review*, 1976, II, No. 2, p. 365 ff.

Gupta, R.K. *Political Thought in the Smriti Literature,* Allahabad, 1961.

Gupte, S.V. *Hindu Law of Marriage*, Bombay, 1976.

Habib, Irfan. 'An Examination of Wittfogel's Theory of Oriental Despotism'. *Enquiry*, 6 pp. 53–73.

Hegel, G.W.J. *Philosophy of History*, trans. J. Sibree, New York, 1949.

Held G.H. *The Mahabharata: An Ethnological Study*, Amsterdam, 1935.

Hobsbawm, Eric. *On history*, Abacus, London, 1997.

Hopkins, E.W. *The Mutual Relations of the Four Castes According to the Manvadharmasastram*, Parlour, Delhi, 1976; Leipzig. 1881.

——. 'Social and Military Position of the Ruling Caste in Ancient India', JAOS, xiiim, 57–376, Bharat Bharti, Varanasi, 1972.

Hutton, J.H. *Caste in India*, Cambridge, 1946.

Jayaswal, K.P. *Hindu Polity*, 2pts. Butterworth, Calcutta, 1924.

——. *Manu and Yajnavalkya*, Butterworth, Calcutta, 1930.

Jha, Chakradhar. *History and Sources of Law in Ancient India*, New Delhi, 1987.

Jha, D.N. *Revenue System in Post-Mauryan and Gupta Times*, Punthi Pustak, Calcutta, 1967

——. 'Early Indian Feudalism: Historiographical Critique', *Presidential Address, Ancient India Section, Indian History Congress, 40th Session.*

Jha, Ganganath. *Hindu Law and Its Sources*, Allahabad, 1930.

Jolly, J. *Arthasatra of Kautilya*, Lahore, 1923.

——. *Hindu Law and Custom*, trans. B.K. Ghosh, Calcutta, 1928.

——. *Outlines of a History of Hindu Law*, Tagore Lectures, Calcutta, 1885.

Jones, Sir William. *Institutes of Hindu Law*, Calcutta, 1877

Kane, P.V. *History of Dharmasastra*, Poona, Bhandarkar Oriental Research Institute, 1930–1946.

Kashyap, Subhash C. *Our Constitution* (2nd ed.), Delhi, National Book Trust, 2011.

Ketkar, S.V. *History of Caste in India*, Ithaca, N.Y., 1909.

Kosambi, D.D. *An Introduction to the Study of Indian History*, Bombay, Popular Prakashan, 1956.

——. *The Culture and Civilization of Ancient India; An Historical Outline*, Routledge & Kegan Paul, London, 1965; Vikas, Delhi, 1970.

——. On the Development of Feudalism in India,' ABORI, xxxvi, 258–59.

——. The Text of the Arthasastra,' *Journal of the American Oriental Society*, LXXVIII (1958).

Kulke, Herman. *Jagannath-kult and Gajapati Konigtum*, Weisbaden, 1979.

——. *Kings and Cults*, Delhi, 1993.

Kuppuswami, B. *A Study of Opinion Regarding Marriage and Divorce*, Bombay, 1957.

Lal, Achhe Dr. *Prachin Hindu Vidhi*, Varanasi, 1981.

Laski, H.F. *Authority in the Modern State*, New Haven, Yale Univ. Press, 1919.

Laski, H.J. *Political Thought in England from Locke to Bentham*, New York, Holt, 1920.

Law, N.N. *Aspects of Ancient Indian Polity*, Bombay, Orient Longman, 1921.

——. *Interststate Relations in Ancient India*, London, 1920.

——. *Studies in Ancient Hindu Polity*, London, 1914.

Lingat, R. *The Classical Law of India*, tr. from French with additions by J. Duncan M. Derrett, University of California, 1973.

Macdonell, A.A. *A History of Sanskrit Literature*, London, 1917.

MacDonell, A.A. and Keith, A.B. *Vedic Index of Names and Subjects*, 2 vols, London, 1912; Delhi, 1967.

Maine, Sir Henry. *Ancient Law*. London, 1866.

——. *Village Communities in the East & West*, London, 1871.

Majumdar, R.C. *Corporate Life in Ancient India*, Firma K.L. Mukhopadhayay, Calcutta, 1969.

——. *Historiography in Modern India*, Bombay, Asia Publishing house, 1970.

Marx, Karl. *Historical Writings*, Bombay, PPH, 1944.

Marx, K. and F. Engels. *On Colonialism*, Moscow, 1968.

Maurya, R.R., *Hindu Law*, Allahabad, 1975.

Mayne, J.D. *A Treatise on Hindu Law and Usage*, (1st ed. in 1878) 16th edition pub. by R.N. Mishra, Delhi, 2008

Mees, G.H. *Dharma and Society*, The Hague, 1935

Mehta, R.N. *Pre-Buddhist India*, Examiner Press, Bombay, 1939.

——. *Crime & Punishment in the Jatakas*, IHQ. Vol, xii, No., p. 438.

Menski, Werner F. *Hindu Law: Beyond Tradition and Modernity*, Oxford University Press, New Delhi, 2003.

Merchant, K.T. *Changing views on Marriage and Family*, Madras, 1935.

Mill, James. *The History of British India*, 2nd (ed.) London, 1820.

Mishra, Srikanta., *Ancient Hindu Marriage Law and Practice*, New Delhi, 1994.

Mitter, D.N. *The Position of Women in Hindu Law*, Calcutta, 1913.

Montesquieu. *The Spirit of Laws*, Trans. T. Nugent, The Hafner, New York. 1949

Mookerji, R.K. *Ashoka*, Motilal Banarsidass, Delhi, 1962; London, 1928.

——. *Local Government in Ancient India*, Oxford, 1920.

——. *Men and Thought in Ancient India*, London, 1924.

——. *Hindu Civilization*, London, 1936.

Motwani, K. Manu: *A Study in Hindu Social Theory*, Dadra, 1937.

Mukherjea, Bijan Kumar. *The Hindu Law of Religious and Charitable Trust*, Calcutta, 1962.

Mulla, D.F. *Principles of Hindu Law*, 13th (ed.) by S.T. Desai, Bombay, 1970.

Müller, Max. *History of Ancient Sanskrit Literature*, London, 1860.

Nehru, Jawaharlal. *Glimpses of World History*, 2 vols., Allahabad, 1934–35.

Nelson, J.H. *Indian Usage and Judge made Law*, London, 1887.

Nelson and Bridges. *Legalizing Gender Inequality*, Cambridge, UK, 1999.

Nilakanta Sastri, K.A. *The Colas*, Madras, 1935–37.

——. *Studies in Chola History and Administration*, Madras, 1932.

——. *The Theory of Pre-Muslim Indian Polity*, Madras, 1912.

Ojha, Dinesh Kumar. *Interpretations of Ancient Indian Polity: A Historiographical Study*, Varanasi, 2006.

Oppenheimer, F. *The State*, New Yourk, 1975 (rept).

Oppert, Gustav. *On the Weapons, Army Organization, and Political Maxims of the Ancient Hindus*, Madras, 1880.

Pal, Radhabinoda. *The History of Hindu Law*, Cal. 1958.

——. *The History of the Law of Primogeniture*, Cal. 1929.

Pannikkar, K.M. *The Origin and Evolution Kingship in India*, Baroda, 1938.

Pannikkar, K.N. *Gulture and Consciousness in Modern India*, New Delhi, *1990*.

——. *Culture, Ideology, Hegemony*, Tulika, New Delhi, 1995.

Pathaka, J.K. and Sharma, B.K. *The Law of Stridhana*, Allahabad, 1998.

Pathak, V.S. *Ancient Historians of India*, APH, 1966.

Patkar, Madhukar. *Narad, Brahaspati and Katyayan: A Comparative Study in Judicial Procedure*, New Delhi, 1978.

Paton, G.W. *A Text Book of Jurisprudence*, Clarendon Press, 1946.

Pawate, I.S. *Dayabhaga: or the Individualization of Communal Property and the Communalization of Individual Property in the Mitakshara Law*, Dharwar, 1945.

Philips, C.H. *Historians of India, Pakistan and Ceylon*, London, 1961.

Popper, K.R. *The Poverty of Historicism*, London, 1957.

Prakash, Om. *Early Indian Land Grant and State Economy*, Allahabad, 1988.

Prasad, Beni. *Theory of Government in Ancient India*, Allahabad, Central Book Depot. 1927.

——. *The State in Ancient India*, Allahabad,The Indian Press, 1928.

Raghavacharirar, N.R. *Hindu Law, Principles and Precedents,* 5th (ed.), Madras, 1965.

Rankin, Sir G.C. *Background to Indian Law*, Cambridge, 1946.

Rapson, E.J. *The Cambridge History, of India,* 6 vols. Cambridge, 1922.

Rawls, J. A *Theory of Justice*, London, OUP, 1973.

Renier, G.J. *History Its Purpose and Method*, Boston, 1950.

Rhys Davids, T.W. *Buddhist India*, London, 1903.

Rice, Stanley. *Hindu Customs and Their Origin*, London, 1939.

——. *The Origins of Caste' Asiatic Review*, XXV.

Risley, H.H. *The people of India,* Calcutta, 1908.

Rowse, A.L. *The Use of History,* London, 1963.

Roy, Ajit Gopal. *Hindu Law (Past and Present)*, Patna, 1960.

Roy, Kumkum. *The Power of Gender & Gender of Power: explorations in early Indian history*, Oxford University Press, 2010.

Sabine, G.H. *A History of Political Theory,* Rev. (ed.), New York, Holt, 1950.

Saletore, B.A. *India's Diplomatic Relations with East,* Bombay, 1943.

——. *Ancient Indian Political Thought and Institutions*, Bombay, 1964.

Saletore, R.N. *Life in the Gupta Age,* Ist (ed.) Bombay, 1943.

Sankararama Sastri, C. *Fictions in the Development of the Hindu Law Texts,* Madras, 1926.

Sankrtyana, Rahul. *History of Central Asia,* Calcutta, 1964.

Sarkar, B.K. *Political Institutions and Theories of the Hindus,* Leipzig, 1922.

Sarkar, G.S. *Hindu Law,* Calcutta, 1940.

Sarkar, Kishori Lal. *Mimansa Rules of Interpretation*, Calcutta, 1909.

Sarkar, S and Munir, J.J. *The Constitution of India with Short Comments*, Allahabad, Alia Law Agency, 2010.

Sarkar, U.C. *Epochs in Hindu Legal History*, Hoshiarpur, 1958.

Sarvadhikari, R.K. *The Principles of the Hindu Law of Inheritance*, Madras, 1922.

Sen-Gupta, N.C. *Evolution of Ancient India Law*, Calcutta, 1953.

——. *Sources of Law and Society in Ancient India*, Calcutta, 1914.

Sen, Priyanath. *The General Principles of Hindu Jurisprudence*, Tagore Law Lectures, 1918.

Senart, Emile. *Caste in India* tr. by Dension Ross from the French, reprinted by Ess Publications, Delhi, 1975.

Service, E.R. *Origins of the State and Civilization: The Process of Cultural Evolution*, New York, 1975

Shamasastri, R. *Evolution of Indian Polity*, Calcutta, 1920

Sharan, Mahesh Kumar. *Court Procedure in Ancient India: on the basis of Dharmasastra Literature*, Delhi, 1978.

Sharma, R.S. *Aspects of Political Ideas and Institutions in Ancient India*, Delhi, 1959/1968.

——. *Lights on Early Indian Society and Economy*, Bombay, 1966.

——. *Shudras in Ancient India*, Motilal Banarsidas, Delhi, (1st ed., 1958) 1990.

——. *Indian Feudalism*, University of Calcutta, 1965.

——. *'Disarming of the Peasants under the Mauryas'*, *Enquiry*, No. 6, 129–33.

——. *Material Culture and Social Formation in Ancient India*, Macmillan, Delhi, 1985.

——. *Urban Decay in India (c. 300 – c. 1000)*, Munshiram Manoharlal, Delhi, 1987.

——. *Origin of the State in India*, University of Bombay, 1989.

——. 'Stages in State Formation in Ancient India', *Social Science Probings*, Vol. 2, No. 1 March 1985, pp. 1–19.

Singh, Shivaji. *Evolution of Smriti Law*, Banaras, 1972.

Singh, Bhagwan. *Pracheen Bharat ke Itihaskar*, Sasta Sahitya Mandal Prakashan, Delhi, 2013.

Sinha, H.N. *Sovereignty in Ancient Indian Polity*, Luzac, London, 1936.

——. *The Development of Indian Polity,* Asia Publishing House, Bombay, 1963.

Sircar, D.C. *Studies in the Political and Administrative Systems in Ancient and Medieval India,* Delhi, Motilal Banarsi Dass, 1974.

Smith, V.A. *The Early History of India from 600 B.C. to the Muhammdan Conquest,* Oxford, 1920.

Smritis, *Brihaspati Smriti,* (ed.) A. Fuhrer, Leipzig, 1879.

——. (The Minor Law of Books Part, I), trans. J. Jolly, *S.B.E.,* Vol. xxxiii, Oxford, 1889.

——. *Manu Smriti,* (ed.) J. Jolly, London, 1887.

——. (The Laws of Manu), trans. G. Buhler, *S.B.E.,* Vol. xxv, Oxford, 1886.

Spellman, J.W. *Political Theory of Ancient India: A study of Kingship from the Earliest Times to Circa A.D. 300,* Clarendon Press, London, 1964.

Spenglar, *The Decline of the West,* London, 1959.

Sreedharan, E. *A Textbook of Historiography* (500 BC to AD 2000), New Delhi, Orient BlackSwan, 2004.

Srinivas, M.N. *Caste in Modern India and Other Essays,* Bombay, 1962.

Sternbach, L. *Judicial Studies in Ancient Indian Law,* Varanasi, 1967.

Supakar, Shraddhakar. *The Law of Evidence in Ancient India,* Calcutta, 1990.

Thapar, Romila. *Ashoka and the Decline of the Mauryas,* London, 1961.

——. *A History of India,* Vol. I, Penguin 1966.

——. *Ancient Indian Social History: Some Interpretations,* Orient Longman, Delhi, 1978

——. *From Lineage to State:* Social formations in the Mid-First Millennium B.C. in the Ganga Valley, OUP, Delhi, 1984

——. *The Mauryas Revisited,* K.P. Bagchi, New Delhi, 1987.

——. *The Past and Prejudice,* National Book Trust, Delhi, 1975.

——. *Cultural Pasts,* OUP, 2000.

Thompson, J.W. *History of Historical Writing,* New York, 1942

Thorner, D. 'Marx on India and the Asiatic Mode of Production', *Contributions to Indian Sociology,* 1966, No. 9, pp. 33–66.

Toynbee, A. *Study of History,* London, (Abridged Edition), 1947.

Trevelyan, Sir E.J. *Hindu Law,* 3rd (ed.) Calcutta, 1929.

Tripathi, H.N. *Pracheen Bharat mein Rajya aur Nyaypalika,* Motilal Banarasidas Publisher, Varanasi, 1993.

Tripathi, L.K. *Position and Status of Women in Ancient India* (ed.) Vol. I and II, Varanasi, 1988.

Varadachariar, Sir S. *The Hindu Judicial System,* Lucknow, 1946.

Varma, Lal Bahadur. *Understanding History,* Allahabad, 1995.

Varma, Vishwanath Prasad. *Studies in Hindu Political Thought and Its Metaphysical Foundations,* Delhi, Motilal Banarasidas, 1954.

Vinogradoff. *Common Sense in Law,* Oxford, U.P. 1947.

Vishwanath, S.V. *International Law in Ancient India,* Longman Green, London, 1925.

Walsh, W.W. *An Introduction to Philosophy of History,* Hutshinson University Library, London, 1951.

Weber, A. *History of Indian Literature,* Trans. J. Mann, London, 1882.

Weber, Max. *The Protestant Ethic and the Spirit of Capitalism* (trans. Talcott Parsons), New York, 1930.

——. *The Religion of India* (trans. H. Gerth and D. Martindale), Glencoe, III, 1958.

West, Sir R. and Buhler, G. *A Digest of the Hindu Law of Inheritance ... 3rd,* and best, edn. Bombay, 1884.

Westermarck, Edward. *The History of Human Marriage,* London, 1921.

Winternitz, Maurice. *History of Indian Literature,* 3, Vols. trans. by Srinivas Sarma, Delhi, Motilal Banarsidas, 1981.

Wittfogel, K. *Oriental Depotism,* New Haven, 1957.

Yadav, B.N.S. *Society and Culture in Northern India in the twelfth century,* Allahabad, 1973.

Yadav, Bhupendra. *Framing History: Context and Perspectives*, Publications Divisions, Ministry of Information and Broadcasting, Govt. of India, New Delhi, 2012.

Journals and Periodicals

ABORS – Annals of the Bhanadarkar Oriental Research Institute, Poona.

IHQ – Indian Historical Quarterly, Calcutta.

IHR – Indian Historical Review, Delhi.

JRAS – Journal of the Royal Asiatic Society, London.

ASB – Journal of the Asiatic Society of Bengal, Calcutta.

JOR – Journal of the Oriental Reseach, Madras.

EPW – Economic and Political Weekly (English Monthly).

Index